NIC AIDEN

Bathing in the Forest

A Healing Guide to Self-Love, Reducing Stress, and Changing Your Life by Connecting with Nature

MOSS & PINE

First published by Moss and Pine Press 2021

Copyright © 2021 by Nic Aiden

All rights reserved. No part of this publication may be reproduced, stored or transmitted in any form or by any means, electronic, mechanical, photocopying, recording, scanning, or otherwise without written permission from the publisher. It is illegal to copy this book, post it to a website, or distribute it by any other means without permission.

Nic Aiden asserts the moral right to be identified as the author of this work.

Nic Aiden has no responsibility for the persistence or accuracy of URLs for external or third-party Internet Websites referred to in this publication and does not guarantee that any content on such Websites is, or will remain, accurate or appropriate.

Designations used by companies to distinguish their products are often claimed as trademarks. All brand names and product names used in this book and on its cover are trade names, service marks, trademarks and registered trademarks of their respective owners. The publishers and the book are not associated with any product or vendor mentioned in this book. None of the companies referenced within the book have endorsed the book.

First edition

*This book was professionally typeset on Reedsy.
Find out more at reedsy.com*

Contents

Introduction	1
The Roots of Forest Bathing	9
A Little About Me	9
The History of Forest Bathing	12
The Significance of Forest Bathing	13
For Those Who Like Science	18
Measuring Stress	22
How Does Nature Do All This?	27
What Other Research is There?	30
The Forest is Calling	34
Prepare for the Internal Journey	36
Prepare for the External Journey	38
Find Your Place of Nature	39
Arrive and Leave Behind	42
Setting an Intention	44
The Birks of Aberfeldy	45
Step into the Forest	49
Give Thanks	49
Leave Nothing but Footprints	50
Tuning in to the Forest's Energy	52
Form Connections	53
Embrace the Weather	54
Stepping into the Threshold	56
Connecting with your Senses	58

Sound	58
Natural Silence	59
Singing with the Trees	63
Connecting with Sound	66
Sight	68
Seeing Fractals	69
Look up	71
Connecting with Sight	73
Smell	76
The Smell of the Forest	76
The Smell of the Earth	79
The Power of Breathing	80
Connecting with Smell	82
Touch	84
Grounding Yourself in Nature	85
Connecting with Touch	88
Taste	91
Foraging Wild Foods	92
Bringing your own food	94
Connecting with Taste	95
The Sixth Sense	97
Connecting with my Sixth Sense	98
Let Nature Guide You	100
Self-Love	100
Following the Signs	102
Finding a Sacred Object	104
Finding Your Own Way	105
How to End Your Forest Bath	107
Thank the Forest	107
Time for Reflection	108
Maintaining the Connection	109

Wandering and Reflecting	110
Growing your own Forest	113
Fill Your House with Plants	113
The Smell of Nature Inside	114
Drinking Herbal Teas	117
Set Your Body to Forest Time	118
Forest Bathing at Work	119
Working in Nature	122
The Future for Us and the Forest	124
The Future of Forest Bathing	128
What can We Do?	129
Sharing is Caring	132
Final Words	134
Moss & Pine Book Club	137
References	138

Introduction

Picture this: you are sitting at your work desk, listening to the sound of people typing away at their computers in the next cubicle. Perhaps you hear distant chatter as someone answers a work call or a frustrated co-worker explains something to a customer. The ping of an email comes from your laptop, and you rush to open it. You're trying to focus, but distractions are all around you. As you read the email and formulate a response, your phone rings. You answer it in a hurry, already exhausted by the customer on the other end of the line, complaining about things outside of your control. As soon as you hang up, a colleague approaches you, looking for a chat and further distracting you from the goal at hand—responding to this email as more and more pile in, one after the other. Stress is building as you worry about meeting your deadline. You don't want to have to work overtime, but it's looking more and more likely.

Miraculously, you manage to get your work done before the end of your shift. Of course, you get no appreciation from your boss for your hard work. You gather your few belongings and begin your commute home. Perhaps you just miss the bus and have to wait for the next one to come, or perhaps the trains aren't running. There are people crowded around you, rushing to get home like you are. Everyone is in a hurry, and no one is getting anywhere. The agitation of the people around you only serves to further your stress, and you fear that you will never make it home. Perhaps you're driving home instead, and traffic is heavy. You get stuck at stoplight after stoplight, your car wedged in between two others, no space for you to move up. You move a few feet every couple of minutes, making no real progress.

Finally, you walk through your front door. Your mind is clouded with the day's stress, your body still tense. Being home doesn't calm your nerves like it used to. You want to cook a meal, but you're too exhausted. You want to see your friends, but you don't have the energy to socialize. Even though you're too exhausted to do anything but sleep, you know that these hours are precious and that you should make the most of them. Even though you want to do something, you are too physically and mentally tired to make an effort. Everything you do only serves to exhaust you further, and nothing can bring you any pleasure. You feel trapped—you want to make the most of the hours before you sleep, but this seemingly endless cycle prevents you from doing that. Every minute is a minute closer to going back to work and reliving the same day once again. You're stuck in a cycle that you cannot escape, and life shows no signs of getting better. Your mental health is deteriorating bit by bit, and you feel that there is nothing left and no way out. How can things get better?

Mustering all of your energy, you go into the backyard. You sit down on the grass and begin to breathe deeply, each breath revitalizing you and calming you. The feel of the grass beneath you is comforting, and the sounds of nature around you bring you peace. Perhaps you hear a bird chirping, or a woodpecker pecking, or a fly buzzing. You may hear animals shuffling about, also winding down for the day. There is a light breeze that tickles your skin, a breath of fresh air. You inhale the air around you deeply, finally away from the stuffiness of the office. You are finally at peace. You open your eyes, taking in the surroundings of your small backyard. You can smell the scent of freshly cut grass and the gentle touch of the soil intermingling with this scent. Leaves fall slowly, surrounding you in a perfect circle. You listen to the sounds of nature and study nearby trees—their shape, their beautiful colour, their texture. The blades of grass continue to brush against your skin in the wind, and fresh, crisp air surrounds you. You keep inhaling and exhaling, and you finally feel like you are at peace.

After a while, you realize that you are unsure how much time has passed since you came outside. Perhaps it has only been a few minutes, or perhaps an hour. You are aware that your heartbeat has slowed, your body has relaxed, and your anxiety has begun to fade. Your breaths are deep; your stress and anxiety are significantly reduced. You are connected with nature and the world around you, and everything, for a moment, is okay. This practice is also known as forest bathing, a perfect way to connect with the life and nature surrounding you. Forest bathing is proven to reduce stress and anxiety levels and can help you unwind after a long, hard day.

Forest bathing is a Japanese practice that has existed for centuries. It is connecting with nature "through our senses of sight, hearing, taste, smell, and touch…by opening our senses, it bridges the gap between us and the natural world" (Li, 2018). Forest bathing has serious health benefits discussed within this book, and it is proven also to aid those suffering from mental health struggles. The biophilia hypothesis helps to explain the benefits of forest bathing and why it can be such a special activity. From the Greek word for "love of life and the living world", the biophilia hypothesis was popularized in 1984 by biologist E. O. Wilson (Li, 2019). Wilson believed that, since human beings evolved in nature, "we have a biological need to connect with it. We love nature because we learned to love the things that helped us to survive. We feel comfortable because that is where we have lived for most of our life on earth. We are genetically determined to love the natural world…this affinity for the natural world is fundamental to our health" (Li, 2019).

The history of forest bathing goes back much further than many people may think; though the term was coined in the past few decades, the practice goes back centuries. There is evidence of forest bathing in haiku poems about nature, and traditional Japanese culture is heavily based on nature, with some rituals dating back as far as the sixth century (Plevin, 2018). These practices focus on one's relationship with nature, which can be deeply spiritual. Currently, there are forest bathing programs available in Japan because of the long practice they have had with forest bathing as a form of therapy. These programs focus more on the spiritual aspect of forest bathing, which is just as important as the scientific aspect. Forest bathing is intuitive, as we naturally know how to connect with nature. Human beings have always been a part of nature, and nature is one of the essential places for all life. People instinctively understand how to forest bathe—what they need to learn is how to get in touch with their sense of wonder for nature (Plevin, 2019).

The biophilia theory focuses on the scientific aspect of forest bathing and why it is so beneficial to de-stressing and improving mental health. Human beings who regularly connect with nature are healthier, happier, and better off than those who spend most of their time indoors (Gascon, et al, 2015).

The main benefits of forest bathing are related to mental health. Forest bathing focuses on the mental wellbeing of those who practice it—specifically stress, depression, and anxiety. Many people use forest bathing as a form of therapy—connecting with nature and basking in it can hold serious therapeutic benefits that many people are unaware of. In broader terms, forest bathing can be considered any activity that allows you to connect with nature and the world all around you. Sitting in or walking through nature can be a simple practice to improve mental health and ground you in reality. Forest bathing has also been shown to have various physical health benefits, and it is not only great for mental health. These benefits will be discussed and analysed throughout this book and will provide proof that forest bathing is effective and helpful.

As someone who practices forest bathing, I cannot begin to speak of how much it has benefited my life. Though I am just an average person with a standard job, I can attest that forest bathing works for me, and I have felt the overwhelmingly positive effects of forest bathing. I have noticed a significant difference in my stress and anxiety levels from before practising forest bathing to now. Forest bathing has made huge changes in my life and is a crucial part of my daily routine. If I can practice forest bathing and feel the benefits, anyone can practice it.

Many people forgo focusing on their mental health in favour of other duties of life. People tend to put things such as their career first and often give to others instead of giving to themselves. It is hard to find time to focus on improving your mental health in today's hectic world. With everything going on around you, you may assume that keeping track of your mental health is unimportant compared to life's other tasks. However, it is more important now than ever to focus on your mental health and wellbeing. The increased use of technology, climate change, global pandemics and polarising values and opinions can all cause stress, anxiety, and depression which can have detrimental impacts on your life and impact your work in various ways. To be a good worker and a giving person, you first have to focus on yourself. Pay attention to your needs and mental health first, and look for ways to improve your wellbeing. Poor mental health impacts your mental wellbeing, your physical body, and your relationships. If you want to have a strong body and strong relationships with others, you cannot forget to pay attention to your mental health. Find ways, such as forest bathing, to maintain your mental health before you are too exhausted.

Nowadays, we live in a society that is more disconnected from nature than ever before. Because of the rise in technology and the higher numbers of people living in urban areas instead of suburban or rural areas, people have forgotten what it means to connect with the life around them. Our disconnect with nature correlates with our decline in mental health, as more people are experiencing mental health struggles than ever before. By simply connecting with nature and using it as a restorative method, people can begin to improve their mental health and get it back to where it once was.

Even if you have neglected to look after your mental health in the past, it is never too late to start paying attention to it. No matter how poor your mental health is, there are always ways to improve it and yourself. Forest bathing is a simple, easily accessible, cheap, and effective way to begin and maintain your journey towards a healthy mind, body, and soul. This book will offer you important details about forest bathing and will begin to show you how important forest bathing is to living a healthy life.

"The clearest way into the Universe is through a forest wilderness." - John Muir

The Roots of Forest Bathing

A Little About Me

Forest bathing has completely shifted my outlook on life and has done wonders for my mental and physical health. I currently live in Edinburgh and am working in front of a computer all day for a telecom company. My work can be exhausting and draining, and I often feel as though all of my energy is depleted at the end of the day. Simple tasks seem more difficult, and I am reluctant to do anything else productive. When you're constantly indoors, you tend to feel drained after a long day. Avoiding nature and ignoring your surroundings can seriously negatively impact your mental health—impacts which I have personally felt.

I grew up in Hong Kong, a concrete jungle. Growing up, I had a severe disconnect from nature, which deeply impacted my mental health, though I wasn't aware of it at the time. I was unaware of the beauty of nature and how it could be beneficial to my health and wellbeing. I could not connect with nature because there was little to no nature around me. All around me was a city—no trees, no forests, no place to retreat into when I needed a break. In many ways, I felt trapped, with no escape. The growth in urban areas, which is predicted to continue over the upcoming years, has pulled people away from nature. Nature is where humans are meant to be, and we are more connected with nature than most realize. Without taking breaks to be in nature, people will continue to feel depleted of energy, stressed, and hopeless.

I learned about forest bathing several years ago during a period where I had a poor work-life balance. I would work until late at night, constantly looking at screens, always mentally exhausting myself. My disconnect from nature was more severe than it had ever been before, and I spent almost no time connecting with the world surrounding me. I was experiencing high levels of stress and anxiety and felt lost and trapped. My mental health was on the decline and showed no signs of improving. I was ready to give up and felt there was no way out of what I was feeling. I didn't know what needed to change, but I knew that I could not continue the same way I was.

During this time, I started taking up new hobbies such as outdoor yoga, hiking, and camping to improve my mental health. The more I did these activities, the more I noticed a significant change in how I viewed the world and approached my work. I wasn't as mentally drained, and my levels of stress and anxiety were significantly reduced. I felt hopeful again, something that I had not felt in a long time. While yoga, hiking, and camping were fun, I noticed that the real reason for my decreased stress is that these activities led me to be outdoors, allowing me to reconnect with nature finally. Practising these techniques used in forest bathing changed my outlook on life and transformed the world around me into something that was not hindering me but pushing me forward. Since then, I have been enthusiastic about forest bathing, and I encourage everyone to take time to forest bathe.

"Adopt the pace of nature: her secret is patience." - Ralph Waldo Emerson

The History of Forest Bathing

Forest bathing has a long, intricate history, specifically within Japanese culture. Forest bathing comes from the Japanese term *shinrin-yoku,* a term created by Tomohide Akiyama in 1982. However, the practice of forest bathing goes back much further than 1982. Historically, Japanese culture and other cultures have always formed a relationship and connection with nature. Japanese culture is largely based on an understanding and deep relationship with nature. *Ikebana,* or the Japanese art of arranging flowers, dates to the sixth century. This practice is largely focused on developing one's relationship with nature (Plevin, 2019).

Japan is rooted in a history that is intrinsically tied with nature, and various rituals and spiritual practices in Japan's history have to do with nature. These practices allow people to realize how their lives are tied to the nature around them and how humans could not exist without it. Japanese culture traditionally believes that *shinrin-yoku* helps you open your senses, closing the gap between you and nature. When you understand and are in tune with nature, you will begin to feel restored (Li, 2019). The Japanese concept of *wabi-sabi* describes the beauty of that which is imperfect, impermanent, and incomplete—this represents humans' deep connection with nature (Plevin, 2019).

In ancient Japan, people honoured spirits that came from nature. These spirits manifested themselves in the forms of rivers, mountains, rocks, and trees. Japanese culture believes in *Yamabushi*, warriors who have existed in Japanese lore for centuries. These warriors live in the mountains, looking for spiritual powers and guidance that they gain through asceticism (Plevin, 2019). Their role is to help people connect with nature, as they believe that nature holds all world truths. Nature can be used as a power to restore, physically and mentally. Japanese culture holds the idea that nature allows one to access their highest and truest form and that it is vital to honour the natural world around you. Through these beliefs, the concept of forest bathing was created.

The Significance of Forest Bathing

Now that you have a basic understanding of the history of forest bathing, you may be wondering why it is still important today. In our modern world, people spend more time indoors than ever before. Virtually everything is done in front of screens—work, play, school, etc. Our world is increasingly switching to online, meaning that many people have less time to connect with the natural world. It is estimated that Americans spend over 90 percent of their time indoors, making the need to connect with the outside world even more urgent (Sherwood, 2019). People nowadays forgo spending time in nature to stay inside, both working and doing their favourite activities such as watching television or playing games. Though these leisure activities are not inherently bad, they take away valuable time that could be spent connecting with the surrounding world.

The growth of technology and urban cities correlates with the steady decline in mental health that doctors have observed over the past few decades. Spending so much time indoors is not good for our brain, which instinctively wants to connect with the nature around us. Our bodies are hard-wired to be connected with nature, as for the majority of human existence, nature is all we have known. Because people spend most time indoors, our mental health has decreased and will likely continue to do so if something doesn't change. Millions of people worldwide struggle with mental health disorders such as anxiety and depression, with many struggling to find a solution for their feelings.

Traditional therapy may not suit everyone—some are not emotionally ready and struggle to open up to a therapist, while others can't find a therapist suited to their needs. Because of this, there is a need for alternate forms of therapy outside of what many consider to be traditional. Forest bathing provides a great alternative to traditional therapy and can be used as a stepping stone towards traditional therapy or as one of several tools to help maintain your mental wellbeing. It's an ideal solution for those looking for a way to improve their mental health but who have not had any success thus far.

The benefits of nature and forest bathing cannot be understated. Human beings are connected to nature in a way that many don't realize—before technology, before cities, before our modern world, everything was done in nature. Human beings existed with other species fully in nature, making even today's humans connected with nature somehow despite spending the majority of our lives indoors. Nature is, ironically, the most natural way of restoration that human beings have. Everyone knows how great it can be to take a break from everything to exist in nature—nature brings us incredible comfort, though many don't know why. Nature can change your mood completely, giving you back your energy and helping you develop a more positive outlook on life. We are instinctively drawn to the natural world and feel happier when we are a part of it (Li, 2019). Nature is one of the most valuable resources that human beings have, but it is still often overlooked for mental health. Beyond helping you to de-stress, nature can positively impact your mental and physical wellbeing.

People who practice forest bathing are generally healthier than those who don't. Being in nature allows us to use all of our senses and doesn't limit us like being indoors does. When we are indoors and working, we typically only use our senses of sight and hearing. Forest bathing, however, connects us with the world around us through our senses of sight, hearing, taste, smell, and touch (Li, 2019). Forest bathing not only helps us be in tune with the world around us—it allows us to connect with ourselves on a deeper level and to understand our wants and needs. Nature is where we restore and repair, and one can only begin their regenerative journey by connecting to nature.

Humans are, and always have been, a part of nature. This is why nature is the ultimate rejuvenating method. As humans, we are a part of nature. When we open our senses, the gap between us and nature is closed, and we can begin to recover (Li, 2019). When humans are in tune with nature, true restorations can begin to take place. No matter how long or short your forest bathing is, you will, in some way, be able to restore through this activity. Forest bathing doesn't have to be sitting and cleansing yourself through nature—it can be walking, hiking, exploring, camping, or anything of the sort. Any way that you are connecting with nature is forest bathing. Forest bathing covers a wide array of topics, all of them holding their benefits to restoring your soul.

Though forest bathing is crucial to restoring your inner self and improving your mental health, it also helps keep you physically in shape. Aside from the benefits of walking in nature to help you stay healthy, forest bathing can counter illnesses such as cancer, strokes, and gastric ulcers; it also helps to boost your immune system, lower your blood pressure, and aid in how much you sleep (Sherwood, 2019). Forest bathing is beginning to be considered a form of non-medical therapy, and many doctors recommend that their patients partake in the activity to improve their mental and physical health. Studies have shown that forest bathing can reduce blood pressure, lower cortisol levels, and improve concentration and memory (Sherwood, 2019). Though forest bathing cannot be considered a treatment for physical illnesses, it can help prevent serious health problems that people may run into later in life.

For these reasons, you should begin to consider forest bathing as a legitimate method of getting and staying healthy. Prioritize yourself and your mental health, and try to practice forest bathing regularly if possible. Even short walks through nature can help you stay healthy, and forest bathing does not have to be a huge commitment. Consider reducing your time spent indoors by forest bathing after a long day or on a weekend. Regardless of your schedule, make sure to find time for forest bathing regularly—it can do wonders for you.

"Our task must be to free ourselves... by widening our circle of compassion to embrace all living creatures and the whole of nature and its beauty." - Albert Einstein

For Those Who Like Science

Forest bathing goes beyond just being spiritual. Though forest bathing is important on a spiritual level, numerous studies have been conducted to understand how forest bathing improves your health and functionality. These studies have proven the importance of forest bathing and have documented many of its positive effects.

In 1990, a speculative investigation in Yakushima was conducted to dive deeper into the phenomenon of forest bathing. This is one of the first studies that focused on looking at forest bathing and its natural effects. Though this research trip was more speculative investigation than scientific inquiry, it showed that forest bathing could be associated with improved mood and higher energy levels (Li, 2019). Despite not providing concrete scientific proof that forest bathing was effective, this investigation still provided scientists with a basic understanding of forest bathing and how it could help people be more healthy. After this investigation, people were aware that there was substantial evidence to show that forest bathing could be a potential form of therapy for many.

In 2004, the scientific investigation into forest bathing truly began. In this year, Dr Qing Li, in collaboration with government agencies and academic organizations in Japan, founded the Forest Therapy Study Group (Li, 2019). The purpose of this group was to figure out why trees made people feel so much better and how forest bathing could positively impact someone's mood. This group was the first real scientific endeavour to understand why forest bathing is so effective and how it can positively impact human beings. In 2006, the Forest Therapy Study group journeyed to the forests in Iiyama. In Iiyama, the group was finally able to demonstrate that forest bathing could boost the immune system, increase energy, decrease anxiety, depression, and anger, and reduce stress by bringing about a state of relaxation (Li, 2019).

Furthermore, studies in Iiyama proved that forest bathing could also lower stress hormones cortisol and adrenaline, lower blood pressure, and increase heart-rate variability (Li, 2019). The studies in Iiyama hugely impacted how people viewed forest bathing. It was no longer merely speculative and spiritual—rather, it was grounded in scientific fact and evidence. Iiyama was the first place in Japan to receive forest-therapy certification, as Iiyama's forests' powers had now been scientifically proven.

Aside from the studies conducted in Iiyama, Li and his colleagues have gathered various other findings regarding the effects of forest bathing. Through further studies, Li and his colleagues have discovered that forest bathing, specifically in males, holds far more benefits than walking in urban areas. Some of these benefits include a decreased pulse rate, a decrease in urinary dopamine (a reduction of stress and cravings), a decrease in urinary adrenaline (a sign of reduced hypertension), an increase in adiponectin in serum (improves regulation of blood glucose levels and fatty acid breakdown), a decrease in negative moods, and an increase in feelings of vigour in middle-aged males with high blood pressure (Li et al., 2016). Forest bathing has shown especially promising results in middle-aged males and females suffering from conditions such as high blood pressure. Forest bathing was proven to significantly help physiological and psychological problems that participants were undergoing, bringing about the question of whether or not forest bathing should be used as a prescribed approach in a clinical setting.

Forest bathing is considered a method of preventing illness and holds benefits for young and middle-aged adults. Forest bathing positively affects cardiovascular functions, specifically in middle-aged subjects with high blood pressure (Li et al., 2016). Blood pressure and heart rate are two of the key targets of forest bathing. The fact that forest bathing can reduce stress levels is hugely beneficial to anyone suffering from cardiovascular issues. Middle-aged adults tend to have higher stress levels and blood pressure, which is part of the reason why forest bathing can be so helpful.

Forest bathing can reduce pulse rates in males and females of all ages. One study found that forest bathing increased scores for vigour while decreasing scores for mental illnesses such as depression and anxiety. Fatigue and confusion were also lessened when participants walked in nature. However, when participants walked in urban environments, the scores for fatigue were increased while the scores for vigour were decreased (Li et al., 2016).

Though other studies on forest bathing have certain limitations, they have consistently found similar evidence to Li's studies. Results of a study conducted by Mark D. Payne and Elias Delphinus showed that the results were statistically significant, which suggested that exposure to the forest environment was likely to have significant benefits for humans, specifically in terms of cardiovascular, immune, and neuroendocrine health (2019). Though similar studies have had low participant numbers, they show the positive effects of forest bathing on the human body. By having the studies controlled and using a comparison between forest and urban environments, they were able to show "a strong correlation between exposure to the forest environment and significant improvements in health and wellbeing" (Payne and Delphinus, 2019).

Further studies have found that *shinrin-yoku* is deeply effective when improving mental health, especially when it comes to anxiety. *Shinrin-yoku* was proven to be an effective approach for depression, anxiety, stress, and anger, and spending time in nature has restorative qualities (Kotera et al., 2020). Forest bathing should be acknowledged for its restorative qualities, and scientists have proven how effective forest bathing is when addressing mental health issues. Beyond helping oneself physically, forest bathing does wonders for mental health and overall wellbeing, and reduced anxiety and stress levels can, in turn, improve your physical health.

> "An experiment is a question which science poses to Nature, and a measurement is the recording of Nature's answer." - Max Planck

Measuring Stress

Stress, in a clinical setting, is typically measured by the Perceived Stress Scale (PSS). The Perceived Stress Scale is "a measure of the degree to which situations in one's life are appraised as stressful" (Cohen et al., 1983). Aside from using the Perceived Stress Scale, studies of forest bathing have also measured various traits that indicate someone is under stress. Measuring cortisol levels is one of the most effective ways to measure stress.

Cortisol is a stress hormone released when we are anxious or under pressure. Similar to our heart rate, cortisol levels are generally self-regulating (Li, 2019). Our body releases stress hormones to help us deal with threats when they arrive or to handle an overly stressful event. Hormone levels will return to normal once the stressor is gone, and your heart rate will go back to normal. Stress can be measured when cortisol is released constantly—cortisol being released steadily can disrupt our body's functions and make us more at risk for various health problems (Li, 2019). Therefore, stress can be measured during and after a stressful situation by charting cortisol levels in the affected individual.

As evidenced in the studies mentioned above, forest bathing can significantly help to reduce stress levels in high-anxiety individuals. Aside from lowering cortisol and adrenaline levels, forest bathing helps to suppress the 'fight, flight or freeze' system and enhance the parasympathetic ("rest and recover") system (Li, 2019). Because it can help balance these systems, forest bathing can be considered a legitimate method to reduce stress levels. Regardless of the cause of stress, forest bathing effectively improves the mental wellbeing of those undergoing high levels of stress and anxiety. In Japan, *shinrin-yoku* is now a regular practice for many looking to manage their stress levels.

Forest bathing can also be beneficial for those who have trouble falling asleep and staying asleep. Studies have found that forest bathing helped participants sleep, partly because it reduces stress and anxiety levels. Since not being able to sleep often happens when you are stressed, many people suffer from a lack of sleep, impacting their physical health. 30-40 percent of working-age men in Japan stated that they regularly could not sleep due to stress, while 40 percent said they sleep less than six hours a night (Li, 2019). Our brain only functions properly when it has gotten a healthy amount of sleep, and sleep can impact how we feel. Without good quality sleep, many other aspects of your health will worsen—including your immune system. Sleep deficiencies are linked to "numerous health problems, including increased risk of heart disease, kidney disease, high blood pressure, diabetes, and stroke" (Li, 2019).

In Iiyama, Li decided to investigate how forest bathing could potentially help people get a better night's sleep. Through his conducted studies, in which participants took walks in the morning and afternoon through the forest, Li found that the participants slept for more than 400 minutes, while their previous average was 383 minutes (Li, 2019). The physical activity of walking through the forest was comparable to how much these participants walked on a regular workday, showing that the amount of physical labour was not the key factor in getting better sleep—rather, it was the fact that this physical labour was conducted in a forest setting.

Forest bathing has been found to improve the mood of those who participate in the activity. *Shinrin-yoku* has shown positive impacts when addressing mood disorders and stress, leading to mental relaxation (Kotera et al., 2020). Li's studies and various other scientific studies showed evidence that forest bathing was connected to a better mood and higher happiness levels. Given that forest bathing is effective in helping to assuage the side effects of mental illnesses such as depression, it is no surprise that forest bathing generally makes people happier. High levels of stress are linked to anxiety and anger issues, along with a depressed mood.

One way that the impact of forest bathing on mood is measured is through the POMS (Profile of Mood States) test, in which participants "are given a list of sixty-five emotions and asked to rate the extent to which they are currently experiencing each one on a scale ranging from 'not at all' to 'extremely'" (Li, 2019). Participants take this questionnaire before and after a forest bathing session to see how their mood has changed due to the activity. This study found that walking anywhere reduces anxiety, depression, anger, and confusion; however, positive effects on vigour and fatigue were only noted when walking through forest environments. To keep track of how your mood has changed due to forest bathing, it is a good idea to use the POMS test or a similar test to measure your mood. Doing this can show you how deeply forest bathing can truly affect your mood and the positive benefits it can have on your life. Even short trips to the forest or in nature can change your mood significantly—you don't have to spend days in the forest for your mood to improve. Even short amounts of time spent in nature can make you happier and healthier.

Along with helping you sleep and boosting your mood, forest bathing helps you to have a healthier immune system. This is one of the most important impacts that forest bathing can have on you, as a healthy immune system can help you ward off illnesses that could significantly impact your life. Our immune system plays a critical role in building our defences against viruses, bacteria, and disease. Stress harms our immune functions, making us more likely to fall ill (Li, 2019). Being frequently ill can increase your stress levels even more, as it interferes with necessary life tasks such as work. By having a poor immune system, you will likely face various other issues that will impact your overall mental and physical wellbeing. Forest bathing's effect on the immune system can be measured by analysing the activity of our natural killer cells. These cells are a specific type of white blood cell that attacks and kills unwanted cells, such as cells carrying a virus (Li, 2019).

Li's studies on forest bathing found that, after spending a few days in the forest, the participants' natural killer cell activity increased from 17.3 percent to 26.5 percent; in addition to this, cell numbers went up from 440 to 661, a 50 percent increase (2019). Other scientists studying forest bathing have concluded that forest bathing leads to a significant increase in the percentage of lymphocytes and monocytes, in addition to a decreased percentage of peripheral blood granulocytes. Lymphocytes are white blood cells that contain natural killer cells, T cells, and B cells. Similarly, monocytes are a type of white blood cell—however, they differ from lymphocytes because their main function is to help fight infection and rid the body of dead blood cells. These percentages show the positive impact of forest bathing on one's health and overall wellbeing and the importance of incorporating forest bathing into your health routine.

> "I felt my lungs inflate with the onrush of scenery - air, mountains, trees, people. I thought: This is what it is to be happy." - Sylvia Plath

How Does Nature Do All This?

Now that you know the key benefits of forest bathing, you may be wondering how it is possible that nature and trees can do all of this. It may be difficult to believe that forest bathing can aid in your sleep, mood, and immune system just by reading the facts. However, there is more science that shows how nature can have such a positive impact on you.

Nature and forest bathing can help improve your sleep, mood, and immune system with phytoncides. Phytoncides are chemicals naturally created by plants and smelling them can help boost your immune system. Forest air is full of phytoncides—they are natural oils within plants and are a key part of a tree's defence system (Li, 2019). Depending on how warm or cold it is, there may be more or fewer phytoncides in the air. The main components of phytoncides are terpenes; terpenes are what you can smell when practising forest bathing (Li, 2019). The major types of terpenes are:

- D-limonene, which has a lemony smell
- Alpha-pinene, which has a fresh, piney smell
- Beta-pinene, which smells similar to basil or dill
- Camphene, which smells like turpentine

Though it is well known that phytoncides can help with depression, anxiety, and stress, many are unaware of how they can also help increase natural killer cell function. Li found the solution to this problem—after incubating natural killer cells with phytoncides for a week, he found that "the results showed that both the NK cell activity and the presence of the anti-cancer proteins perforin, granzyme A and granulysin had increased" (Li, 2019). When tested in humans, Li's studies showed that phytoncides being inhaled increases the number of natural killer cells, along with natural killer cell activity.

The activity of anti-cancer proteins was also enhanced in this study. In addition, phytoncides were found to decrease the levels of stress hormones, increase hours of sleep, decrease scores for anxiety, anger, and confusion, cause a pleasant mood, lower blood pressure and heart rate, increase heart-rate variability, and suppress sympathetic nervous activity (Li, 2019). The components of phytoncides allow them to "mediate the stimulatory effect on sympathetic activity" (Kawakami et al., 2004). Studies have shown that phytoncides could help reduce the sympathetic responsiveness that some people may experience under stress; for this reason, phytoncides inhaled during forest bathing contribute to the activity's effect on stress levels.

Microbes also contribute to why forest bathing can be beneficial to human health. Microbes are found in soil, and we breathe them in when we walk through the forest or participate in other forms of forest bathing. The substance in the soil that we breathe in is scientifically known as *Mycobacterium vaccae,* which is a harmless bacteria. Studies have shown the benefits of this bacteria in humans, such as a study conducted by oncologist Dr Mary O'Brien. O'Brien discovered that, though she could not find evidence that *Mycobacterium vaccae* helped fight off illness, injecting the bacteria improved her patients' overall quality of life (Li, 2019). Studies on mice have shown that microbes do have some impact on the immune system and are not just able to help aid in mental illness. *Mycobacterium vaccae* in the soil can help boost our immune system, which makes us happier in general. Though there are various microbes aside from bacteria, such as fungi, archaea, algae, lichens, and viruses, the microbes found in the forest are safe and harmless to human beings. Microbes do many positive things for people, including but not limited to:

- Boosting the immune system
- Protecting us from dangerous pathogens
- Protecting us from auto-immune diseases
- Keeping us in shape
- Detoxifying and lowering stress levels
- Keeping babies healthy

These benefits of microbes can be gained through forest bathing regularly (Torgovnick May, 2012). This is further proof that forest bathing should be considered a legitimate way of getting and staying healthy and that reconnecting with nature is one of the most important things you can do for yourself. Find a way to incorporate nature into your everyday activities—you will be glad that you did so.

What Other Research is There?

A study conducted by Roger Ulrich, entitled "View Through a Window May Influence Recovery From Surgery," has also been integral to our modern understanding of how forest bathing works and of how nature is a great restoration method. Within this study, Ulrich analysed the therapeutic impact of nature on patients recovering from surgery. It has been theorized that, given that patients are confined to their hospital room, their recovery process will be smoother if they are in a room with a window. Viewing the outdoors is important to people with busy schedules who are spending most of their time in the same room, such as surgical patients. Having a view outside can significantly influence a patient's emotions, which may, in turn, help their recovery (Ulrich, 1984).

This study can be considered one of the prime pieces of evidence that forest bathing—or any real interaction with nature, no matter how big or small—can help one restore both physically and mentally. Through this research, Ulrich found that, compared to the wall-view group, patients who could see outdoors had less negative evaluative comments from those treating them. In addition, patients with a window took less moderate and strong analgesic doses and had lower scores for post-surgical complications (Ulrich, 1984). Therefore, even by simply looking out of a window, interacting with nature holds many regenerative properties for individuals enduring emotional or physical stress and exhaustion. Though this study did find that there were not huge differences in the recovery process of those with a window room and those with a wall room, it did show that, in some way, nature affects the recovery process. If this recovery had been taken outside, fully immersed in nature, it would likely show even more promising results than simply looking out of a window. Recovery in nature in situations such as this is not possible—however, for those looking to regenerate mentally and emotionally and those who have come home to recover from a physical injury, being a part of nature can be extremely beneficial.

It is also important to understand the relationship between human health and trees. Put simply, trees help humans stay alive and bring us happiness—not only because they help to produce the air that we breathe, but because we are so deeply connected with nature at our core. The relationship between human health and trees has been studied for decades—when trees die, people die in turn. Humans and trees have a similar average lifespan of 80 years, and both trees and the human body consist mostly of water (Davis, 2012).

Besides these physical similarities, trees and humans have a much deeper connection. Humans and trees have a symbiotic relationship—they need one another to breathe and live (Davis, 2012). The symbiotic relationship human beings have with trees is part of what makes forest bathing so special. As humans give, trees take, and as trees take, humans give—it is an endless cycle, one that keeps humans happy, rejuvenated, and healthy. For these reasons, the importance of incorporating forest bathing into your daily or weekly routine cannot be understated. Forest bathing has the power to change you both physically and mentally—and the science to back it up.

FOR THOSE WHO LIKE SCIENCE

"Nature is not a place to visit. It is home." - Gary Snyder

The Forest is Calling

Now that you understand the scientific benefits of forest bathing, it is time to start preparing for it. To begin, you should start by deciding on a time and place. Choose a time where you will not feel rushed—the stress of feeling rushed will take away from the benefits you can gain from the experience. Analyse the obstacles that you feel are getting in your way.

If you feel short on time or experience troubles on the way to your chosen location, that is okay. Remember to "look deep inside and trust that you already have everything you need, and keep moving forward toward the forest" (Plevin, 2019). All of the tools you need to have a successful journey are already inside of you—you just have to search for them and believe that you have them within you. Because we are so connected to nature- forest bathing, once practised enough, becomes second nature to us.

"These people have learned not from books, but in fields, in the wood, on the river bank. Their teachers have been the birds themselves, when they sang to them, the sun when it left a glow of crimson behind it at setting, the very trees, and wild herbs." - Anton Chekhov

Prepare for the Internal Journey

As you begin your journey, make sure that you are mentally prepared for everything that will come. Beyond going on a physical journey to your chosen location, forest bathing transports you on an inner journey to places you've never discovered. To prepare for the inner journey that forest bathing will take you on, you should begin by being mindful of everything around you—including your dreams, emotions, fears, and any mental images that may arise (Plevin, 2019).

Consider keeping a journal of everything you are feeling to help you practice mindfulness. Keep these feelings to yourself for now—you must put yourself at the centre of the journey and know that this is an experience meant to help you and only you. Other people can go on their internal journeys when they are forest bathing—this one is just for you.

Consider meditating before, during, and after your forest bathing experience. Meditating is a great way to connect with yourself and your emotions, and if you are having trouble putting all of your emotions into cohesive thoughts, meditating will help you do so. Simply being able to notice your emotions and feelings can change how you experience forest bathing.

When you are going on your forest bathing journey, you must have an open heart and mind. Consider asking yourself questions such as how your heart is feeling, why you feel you are being called to connect with Earth and nature, and how you can stay humble while receiving the gifts that forest bathing offers you (Plevin, 2019). Listen to your heart, and process your emotions. Accept every thought that passes through your mind, regardless of what it is. Let yourself feel nature and focus on what it tells you and how it makes you feel. Doing this will significantly impact your experience and make it a more pleasant journey overall. If you're looking to use forest bathing to help your mental state, then you must keep your heart and mind open to any thoughts, feelings, or compulsions that may overcome you. Again, consider keeping a journal to track all of these feelings if your heart tells you that journaling will help process everything. Make sure you are going into your forest bathing experience with good intentions. If you go into it hoping to gain something positive from the experience, nature will reward you. Commit yourself to the Earth around you, and open yourself up to it. Nature will be there to support your journey and to help you connect with the world around you.

In addition to all of these factors, keep in mind that you need to find the right place and time for forest bathing. Find a place in nature that makes you feel safe and comforted—one that is not dangerous and will not keep your mind anxious. Transitional times of the day, such as the liminal hours at dawn or dusk, are especially effective when you begin practising forest bathing as they are periods of change and reflect the transformation you are about to embark on (Plevin, 2019). Offer yourself to Earth, as well as any physical objects you may bring on your journey. If you open yourself up to the Earth around you, it will listen and give back everything you are putting in.

Prepare for the External Journey

Now that you know the importance of your internal journey during forest bathing, you can better prepare for the external journey that forest bathing will take you on. Prepare your body before you go forest bathing by doing simple activities such as drinking water, eating healthy foods, avoiding alcohol, exercising, stretching, and nourishing your body (Plevin, 2019). Wear comfortable clothes when you are going out forest bathing—something that you don't mind getting a bit dirty. You must be as comfortable as possible when you are forest bathing. If you are not comfortable in your body or your clothing, then forest bathing will not be as impactful of an experience for you as it could be. Don't worry about appearances—do what makes you the most comfortable because this journey is all about you at the end of the day. Appearances don't matter when you are connecting with nature. Make sure your clothing is suitable for the forest before venturing out on your journey.

It is also important to keep a backpack of anything you need for safety, mindfulness activities, hydration, and snacks. Some things that you can bring with you on your forest bathing journey include:

- A first aid kit—and know how to use everything in it
- A whistle to call out if you are disoriented after forest bathing
- Water bottle and healthy snacks
- A cloth to lie or sit on
- A journal and a pen to help you practice mindfulness and be aware of what you are feeling during your journey

- Essential oils
- Sun protection
- Cornmeal, birdseed, or anything natural for offerings to Earth
- Soft-soled shoes
- Layers and a raincoat in the event of changes in weather
- A watch to keep time—this helps you avoid looking at your phone
- A musical instrument to help you connect with the Earth
- A phone, only to be used in case of emergency—do not use your phone in other situations as it will distract you from your forest bathing journey (Plevin, 2019)

In addition to these items, ensure that you take other safety precautions. Tell someone where you will be going, and share your location with them from your phone if you feel that it could be necessary. Always make sure that someone knows where you are when you are forest bathing, and give them an estimated period for when you will be done. Research the area you will be going to—know the trails and any wildlife that populate the area, and make sure that it is safe to practice forest bathing. If the location is relatively unknown or you arrive and feel uneasy about it, find somewhere else where you feel safer and more protected. If you do not feel safe in the area where you will be forest bathing, the experience will not benefit you.

Find Your Place of Nature

Finding a place is, once again, vital to your forest bathing experience. Ensure that you feel safe and consider scoping out the area before you go forest bathing. If you have been practising forest bathing in one location and want to try someplace new, you should still make sure that this new place is safe, even if you are skilled in forest bathing.

Against popular belief, forest bathing doesn't have to be a wilderness trek. Forest bathing doesn't even have to take place in the forest, despite what the name implies. Forest bathing is simply the process of connecting with nature, whatever that may entail for you. You can forest bathe wherever there are trees, no matter the weather. If you have a favourite type of landscape that you feel will be the most relaxing, then seek out places that fit this landscape. One of the most important parts of location is making sure you are practising forest bathing in a place that will allow you to engage with all five senses (Li, 2019). Find a place that will relax you and improve your mood, one of the most important aspects of forest bathing. You can forest bathe anywhere—in a park, in your garden or backyard, on a local walk, or anywhere else in nature that will help you to relax.

If you don't live near a forest but still want to practice forest bathing, you do not need to worry. Even if you live in the city, there are areas you can go to that will allow you to forest bathe. Many cities have parks, big and small. These same cities often have gardens, wild areas, and woods; an example of this would be Central Park in New York City, Hyde Park in London, and the Bois de Boulogne in Paris (Li, 2019). These parks allow you to be surrounded by nature and trees, and even if they are crowded, there are typically quiet areas that you can find to meditate and be one with nature. If you live in a big city, don't use this as an excuse not to practice forest bathing—there are plenty of places to be found, even in the most densely populated areas. Cities such as Chicago have various parks surrounded by trees and a lake that you can visit to connect with nature. As you can see, there is no shortage of opportunities to connect with nature, even in the city—it's all about how hard you look and how much you want to practice forest bathing.

> "In every outthrust headland, in every curving beach, in every grain of sand, there is the story of the earth." - Rachel Carson

Arrive and Leave Behind

Once you've found the right place, it is time to make the journey there. Simply showing up at your location is arriving at the destination—those who arrive are meant to be on the journey of forest bathing. Once you arrive, be confident that you are in the right place. Your instincts directed you to this place for a reason, so you shouldn't have any doubts about its power.

As you begin to settle in, it is time to release your emotions. Start by shaking it out, whether that be mentally or physically. Whatever you feel when you first arrive, it is time to let it go. Any thoughts troubling your mind can wait until you have connected and found peace with the Earth. Whatever you are feeling or thinking should not bother you at this moment—simply let go and be one with nature. Allow yourself to turn off what you are feeling, even if it is just for a brief time. Doing so will give you the strength to deal with these troubling emotions later once you have found calm through nature.

It is important that when you are practising forest bathing, you disconnect from everything in the world around you. Turn off your phone, or at the very least, silence any notifications that you might get. Allow yourself to exist away from technology for some time, and use this as an opportunity to focus on what is important in your life. Technology shouldn't be at the centre of your life, but it often is for many attached to their phones. When you become too dependent on your phone, you forget about everything else around you. Forest bathing is the perfect opportunity to put your phone away and realize that things in the world matter more—such as being one with everything and everyone around you.

Continue practising mindfulness when you are forest bathing. Be mindful and present to the natural world around you. Try not to focus on things that do not matter, and listen to nature.

Nature is a great teacher of patience and practice, and if you listen to it, you will find that things are much simpler than they may seem to be. You can come to nature with any questions you may have, and by focusing on being mindful and present, you will get the answers you are searching for. Whatever has been troubling you, nature is there to help you deal with your difficult emotions. Nature listens, and you simply have to listen to it back.

Setting an Intention

When you go to the forest to practise forest bathing, you must have pure intentions. Everything in life begins with intentions. Intentions are vital to the universe. They are turned into words that lead to the manifestation of thoughts and actions—so make sure you are clear with your intentions when forest bathing (Plevin, 2019). Your intention can be simple, such as relaxing, or something more complex, such as finding the answer to a question that you cannot figure out. Regardless of what it is, know what you are looking to get out of your forest bathing experience.

There is a deep relationship between intentions, spirituality, and the universe at large. When we can clearly think of what we want from something and put that intention into practise, we invite the universe to work with us. By knowing what you want, you are calling the universe to help you achieve this goal. If your intentions are pure, then the universe will help you to make them come true. Be at one with the universe and the world surrounding you—this is integral to having a successful forest bathing experience. By knowing that the universe is listening to you when you put your intentions out there, you can get the full benefits from forest bathing that you are searching for.

Begin manifesting your intention by saying it out loud. It is vital that you do this, either to yourself or to others, as "our thoughts can be convoluted and complicated. When we voice our intention, we force ourselves to get clear. The more clear and concise our intention, the better" (Plevin, 2019). Make sure that your intention is clear, and the universe will reward you in turn. Once you have stated your intention, it is then time to let it go. Stop thinking about your intention once you say it aloud. While it may worry you to let go of your intention so swiftly, this is the best way to make intentions work.

Putting all of these steps of your forest bathing journey together does not have to be difficult. In all of my time practising forest bathing, I have learned about the importance of each of these steps and can tell you that you shouldn't skip any of them—all of them are equally valuable and can completely impact your forest bathing experience. Make it as simple or complex as you want it to be, but most importantly, make it your own.

* * *

The Birks of Aberfeldy

Join me on one of my forest bathing trips to the Birks of Aberfeldy, about a two-hour drive from Edinburgh. I go on a Saturday morning and plan my day around the journey. Setting a day aside for forest bathing helps to ensure that you will not feel rushed. While I am on my way to the Birks of Aberfeldy, I begin to prepare myself for my internal journey. As I drive through all of the beautiful scenery surrounding me, taking in nature and immersing myself in it, I start to notice how the stress and anxiety I have faced during the week has been affecting me and my relationships with family and friends. I've been exhausted, on edge, and overworked, and memories of the previous week come flooding back to me. As I picture the events of the week, I focus on how I will be able to escape from the stress I've been feeling by simply embarking on this journey. I open myself up and allow myself to be excited for my forest bathing journey and what it may bring me. The week's stress will not matter any longer—I will finally reach the calm I am searching for.

To prepare for my external journey, I have readied my body to ensure that the forest bathing experience is as pleasant as possible. I haven't drunk alcohol recently, and I have recently eaten a healthy meal and drank a plentiful amount of water. I feel rejuvenated, strong, and ready for whatever lies ahead of me today. My bag is packed with all of the essentials, starting with some healthy snacks—today, it's a homemade sandwich and some cut-up vegetable sticks, a perfect light meal to keep me energised during my forest bathing trip. I pack extra water to make sure that I stay hydrated throughout the whole experience. I bring my journal along with me so that I can write anything down that I may notice or feel and so that I can keep track of everything going on in the forest around me. Using my journal to document my experience will help me in the future and give me a sense of calm when I cannot make the full journey for forest bathing. I pack my first aid kit last and make sure I have all of the essentials in case they are necessary. Once I've finished packing everything, I tell my partner where I will be to be extra safe and cautious.

As I arrive at the Birks, I allow myself to shake off any emotions from the past week, mentally and physically. As I do this, I let go of everything I have been feeling and breathe in the crisp air surrounding me. Now, I am prepared to see where my journey takes me. I switch my phone off to avoid any distractions that may arise while I am in nature. Finally, I set my intention—I want to be open and mindful, but I don't want to criticise myself if I cannot be open and mindful. Regardless of achieving my intention, I accept that it is all part of the practice and the journey. No matter what happens, I am improving myself by going on my forest bathing journey. I take a deep breath, inhaling as much air as I can, holding it, and letting it out. It is time—I am ready to enter the forest.

"I like this place and could willingly waste my time in it."
- William Shakespeare

* * *

Step into the Forest

Give Thanks

Now that you have prepared yourself for the journey, it is time to begin forest bathing. Start by giving thanks to the forest and the nature and life surrounding you—it is all there to help you along your journey. Giving these words of thanks helps to create the connection between you and the forest and allows you to build a relationship with everything around you. Since you have decided on your intentions, it is important to communicate them to the forest. State what you are looking to get from this experience. You can also say a prayer for the forest's protection, for everything that inhabits it, and for all who are journeying into the forest for the same reasons that you are—you are a part of something greater, a web of living things, and you protect each other (Plevin, 2019). All these actions can deepen the relationship. Once you have established this connection, it is time to dive deeper into your forest bathing journey.

Leave Nothing but Footprints

When you are forest bathing, you must take care of the forest. Though it should go without saying, make sure that you are not littering or damaging the plants and surrounding life. Don't cross any barriers that will harm the forest—you are there to take care of it in the same way it is taking care of you. Give the forest what you want to get back from it—this is a mutual relationship and should have mutual respect. If you want to pick flowers, forage berries, or do other activities while forest bathing, make sure that you first ask for permission. While this may sound silly, it is a sign of respect, and the Earth will appreciate your asking.

As a side note, make sure you know what food you are picking if you decide to engage in activities such as foraging for berries. If you do not know what you are doing or what food you are picking, you are putting yourself in danger—so make sure you are absolutely positive that you know what you are doing. Consider having a guide to what foods in the forest are edible and what will and won't hurt you if you ingest them. Be respectful of the nature around you, and appreciate all it has to offer for you. Know that you are blessed to be here now—and remember to leave nothing but footprints.

As you begin to walk, feel the earth below your feet, and experience how you interact with the world changes. You should walk barefoot when you are forest bathing—though this is not always possible, walking barefoot allows you to absorb the energy coming from the earth. Walking barefoot allows you to absorb electrons into your body and neutralize and release toxic free radicals (Ober, et al., 2014). By walking barefoot, you help to calm your nervous system and allow your body to return to an electrical state (Plevin, 2019). Allow yourself to fully connect with the world around you—it is all there for you, and you should be thankful for this. Respect the earth surrounding you, and bask yourself in its beauty. Now that you have created the connection between you and the forest and stated your intentions, you can ask for further protection and build the relationship between you, the forest, and the universe.

"Trees are always a relief, after people." - David Mitchell

Tuning in to the Forest's Energy

While you are in the forest, energy is all around you. Begin by cultivating the energy of the trees. A tree's vascular system expands to pump water up into the tree, similar to how our heart pumps blood through our body (Plevin, 2019). Because we have such a close-knit relationship with the earth, this energy comes back into us. As the trees release energy, we take that energy in. The forest allows us to be surrounded by trees and acts as a vast energy source. There are various ways to absorb the energy and tap into it when you are forest bathing. Find the right way for you, whether sitting and meditating, walking barefoot, giving offerings to the forest, or slowly breathing in the air around you. The basics of forest bathing—breathing and mindfulness—are among the best ways to feel the earth's energy surrounding you.

Form Connections

There are many ways that you can connect with the trees and plants surrounding you. Feel the energy of the trees all around you. Awareness of energy, or life force, is an old belief that continues until this day. This awareness is known as *qi* in China and *prana* or *shakti* in India. Qigong is the ancient Chinese practice of balancing your qi and gaining life energy as a method of staying healthy and feeling revitalized (Plevin, 2019). This practice can be done with any form of nature, including trees, plants, or stones. It is best to start with trees when you are first practising qigong. There are steps you can take to practise these beliefs.

1. Pay attention to everything around you. If there is a particular tree that you are drawn to, ask its permission to touch it and interact with it.
2. Find the tree that you connect to the most. Ask it for permission to give it love. Take deep breaths, and focus on radiating loving energy from your heart and giving it

to the tree. The tree will give back to you what you are giving to it.
3. Inhale the energy from the tree, letting it radiate through your body. Now exhale the energy back into the tree, and do this action once again.
4. Exhale energy from your heart up to the sky. Inhale it back into your own body. Do this for as long as you would like (Plevin, 2019).

Embrace the Weather

Once you have completed this practice, it is time to move on to embracing the weather. Whether it's rain or shine, you should appreciate what nature has to offer. If it is sunny out, begin by greeting the sun. The sun is our power source, and we could not exist without it. When the body feels sunlight on the skin, it sends a message to slow melatonin production, a sleep-promoting hormone, while increasing serotonin levels, which elevates mood (Plevin, 2019). The sunlight is part of the reason we experience happiness, and if you are forest bathing on a sunny day, make sure that you are appreciating and communicating with the sun. Let it soak into your skin, and take deep breaths to connect with it. The sun gives us life and energy, so soak up as much of that energy as you can.

If it is windy or rainy outside, you can still take the opportunity to appreciate the weather. Regardless of your favourite type of weather, everything is a part of nature and should be valued for that reason. Feel the wind on your skin from the breeze, or let the drops of rain fall upon you. Appreciate everything around you. Even cloudy or rainy, the sun is still there, shining down on you above the clouds. To greet the sun, follow these steps:

1. Begin by facing the sun, with your palms facing towards the sun as well.
2. Bring your hands together over one another, creating a triangular shape.
3. Close your eyes and stay still. Feel the sun shining down onto your skin, and accept its energy into your body.
4. Inhale, and put your hands in a prayer position. Feel the energy radiating from the sun.
5. On your next inhale, circle your arms and bring them back in front of you. Repeat these movements as many times as you would like until you can feel the sun warming your body and heart and providing you with energy.
6. Say your affirmations to the sun. You can do this by saying the date and your name, then thanking the world for being able to connect to the universe around you. If you feel any premonitions, be sure to take note of them.

These methods are ways to increase and encourage mindfulness, being present, and reconnecting with nature. It is important to take all these steps to have the best forest bathing experience possible. If you are truly dedicated to connecting yourself with the earth, then using these rituals will help you feel at peace with your surroundings.

* * *

Stepping into the Threshold

I try to engage in these practices as much as possible when I am forest bathing. I have found that they are incredibly helpful when connecting myself with the beauty of the world surrounding me. Continuing with my forest bathing trip at the Birks of Aberfeldy, I begin by walking to the edge of the forest, making a note of the ground beneath my feet, the crisp air entering my lungs, and the sun warming my skin. I find a natural opening between two trees where I will feel the sunlight shine down on me. I look up to the sky. It's a cloudy day with a nice breeze that is cooling the warmth on my skin. Even though it is hard to see the sun right now, I know it is still there. I feel the wind on my face and embrace the energy that it brings me. I take a deep, long breath, hold it, then exhale. I do this again and again, centring myself and connecting myself to everything around me.

I continue by walking up to a tree that I am drawn to by following the process detailed earlier. Once I approach it, I ask for its permission to give me the energy I am searching for. If the tree does not permit me, I find another one. I put my hand on its trunk, feeling the coarseness of the bark under my skin. The bark is textured, rough but appealing all at once. I close my eyes, and I begin to thank the nature around me and the tree that provides me with energy. I breathe deeply and share energy with the tree. Connecting myself to the tree and the forest, I continue to take deep, steady breaths. Once I am done, I feel the energy coursing through my body. I am at peace, and I can rest easy knowing that my journey was a success.

"Love trees until their leaves fall off, then encourage them to try again next year." - *Chad Sugg*

* * *

Connecting with your Senses

When you are forest bathing, you must connect with all five senses. Sound, sight, smell, touch, and taste. Make sure that you are in tune with everything around you, and take note of everything you feel. Consider going through the senses and listing in your head what you are noticing in the forest around you.

Sound

There are many noises that we hear daily, some more pleasant than others. If you are in a city, you constantly hear the noise of everything happening around you, whether it be honking cars on the street, the whooshing of a train going by, or the constant chatter from people walking downtown. Noise anywhere can become overwhelming for people, and sometimes, all you want is to escape it. Though cities can be exciting to live in, they are stressful because of the noise surrounding you. Everything in a city is constantly moving, and there is no time for rest or relaxation, no escape from the incessant noise. Noise is beyond annoying—it can also "increase blood pressure, interfere with concentration and sleep and lead to forgetfulness" (Li, 2019).

Noise pollution is one of the most damaging environmental threats to health. The World Health Organization found that up to 1.6 million life-years were taken off in Western Europe due to noise pollution (Göransson, 2021). Cities are taking various preventative measures to deal with the growing issue of noise pollution, which continues to worsen in places that are not working to combat it. Many cities are using technology that can tell when a decibel threshold is broken. However, these devices are limited in scope, as they typically cannot pinpoint the source of the noise or understand what is causing a specific sound (Göransson, 2021). Many cities are not conscious of their noise pollution, which is making the issue worsen.

The best way to analyse noise in cities is by using acoustic sensors and monitors—by utilizing many small, high-quality microphones, an acoustic sensor creates accurate visualizations of where sounds are coming from—smart cities can pinpoint the source of certain noises (Göransson, 2021). By using this technology, cities can analyse the noise source and take corrective measures to lessen the volume of the noise. Other cities are using smaller methods of quieting the noise, such as "quiet concrete," which dampens the sound of traffic, issuing fines for noises above certain decibels, specifically for motorcycles, and implementing leaf blower regulations (Cournoyer and Fetterman, 2018).

Natural Silence

The importance of natural silence cannot be understated—however, most people no longer have a chance to enjoy the sounds of peace and quiet. Natural silence is thought of as one of the most endangered resources in the world—in fact, silence has become such a rarity that the US National Park Service put a protection order on it (Li, 2019). In the Olympic National Park in Washington, in the middle of the Hoh Rainforest, a red stone marks a square inch of silence—part of a campaign to create places free of man-made noise (Li, 2019). This rainforest, along with many other forests, provides the perfect opportunity for people to escape from artificial noise that typically bombards them. This spot is the quietest place in America to inspire more places to be dedicated to silence.

Though you may think natural silence needs to be the absence of any noise, this is not necessarily true. Natural silence does not always mean complete and utter silence. When you are forest bathing, you experience natural silence, regardless of the surrounding sounds. Natural silence is meant to detach you from the sounds of human noises, allowing you to connect with what you hear in nature and make a note of sounds that aren't overwhelming to your senses. Recording natural sounds can also help you find moments of natural silence amid loud noise surrounding you.

The Ministry of the Environment in Japan, for example, recorded a hundred sounds from Japan. Some of these sounds included noises from the Sagano bamboo forest (Li, 2019). The Ministry of the Environment in Japan has created various sounds that people can listen to, preserving natural silence. While you are in nature, you can preserve natural silence as well, either through recording the sounds around you or simply remembering them so that you can reflect on them later. When you are free from man-made noise, you can finally listen to the sounds of nature and everything it has to offer.

Listening to natural sounds is an important part of forest bathing. You can take in natural sounds and natural silence by taking a walk through the forest. As you pay attention to all of your senses, take note of all of the sounds you hear and how they differ from man-made sounds. The sounds of nature are much more gentle and don't hurt the ears in ways that man-made sound does. Pay attention to the sound of the wind, the leaves under your feet, the call of birds around you—anything that you can hear in nature. Find a place as removed from manufactured noise as possible—when you are free of this, you can enjoy natural silence.

Urban sounds, aside from having negative impacts on our hearing, also lead to a host of mental and physical problems. Loud noises can make sleeping more difficult, which negatively impacts your health—if you do not have sound sleep health, you may run into various physical and mental problems. However, aside from hurting your sleep health, noise pollution in cities is linked to many other issues. According to the World Health Organization (WHO), urban noises can lead to cardiovascular disease, cognitive impairment, and high levels of stress—on average, at least one million life years are lost every year due to traffic-related noises, specifically in western Europe (Jaffe, 2015). In addition to these issues, those living in cities tend to have more mental illnesses, more addictions, more depression, and more anxiety (Li, 2019). WHO considers stress an epidemic of the twenty-first century, and finding ways to manage stress is becoming increasingly important.

In contrast, listening to natural sounds while forest bathing is beneficial for physical and mental health. Even small amounts of time spent forest bathing can positively impact our health. Forest bathing, as mentioned before, holds the power to reduce stress levels, reduce blood pressure, improve cardiovascular functions, lower blood-sugar levels, lift depression, improve concentration, improve energy, boost the immune system, and increase anticancer protein production (Li, 2019). Exposure to natural sounds specifically provides health benefits when in comparison to urban noises. In parks, noise exposure degrades our enjoyment and health, as it is an environmental stressor (Buxton et al., 2021). In addition, as populations become more urbanized and people are exposed to more noise pollution, "experiencing soundscapes rich in natural sound without noise will become even more exceptional and important for enhancing the health of visitors" (Buxton et al., 2021). Therefore, forest bathing and being one with nature is much healthier than constantly being in urban areas. If you live in a city, you must get away from it all and find a way to forest bathe. The sounds of nature will not harm your hearing, and listening to the world around you can help you stay happy and healthy.

> *"At one time in the world, there were woods that no one owned." - Cormac McCarthy*

Singing with the Trees

There are various ways that you can use sound to connect with nature. One of these methods is singing with the trees. Though it may sound like something you would be too shy to do, it's worth a shot. Regardless of your relationship with your voice, you can gain a lot by singing with the trees. Singing can help you connect with yourself and to merge yourself with the rest of the world. Earth songs have been passed down through generations, and every culture connected to nature practices them (Plevin, 2019).

Using some of these traditional songs or creating songs of your own is an amazing way to make yourself one with the earth. The sound of music while singing to the melodic noises of nature around you can be calming and benefit your health. Singing on your own in the forest is a great example of combining man-made and natural sounds to create soothing noise that will improve your health. Your song can be about anything—a journey, restoring, celebrating, remembering, being hopeful, or anything that you think will be useful to sing about (Plevin, 2019).

As you sing your song to the trees, pay attention to everything else that you hear around you. The forest is playing its music, with the sound of running water, birds chirping to one another, your feet hitting the ground—any sound that can be heard during your forest bathing experience can be considered music in and of itself. Sing your thanks to the earth around you, and express your deep gratitude for everything it is offering you. Sing what is on your mind as you make your journey, or sing the sounds that you hear in the forest. Sing a prayer that you want to offer up to the trees. Anything that you give, nature will reciprocate. Try singing and see how nature sings back to you. You can also consider bringing an instrument of your own to play along with your singing. Let out what you are

CONNECTING WITH YOUR SENSES

feeling or what emotions have been building up in you in your day-to-day life. Whatever you have been holding back, it is time to release.

You must know how to be still and listen to the sounds of nature around you when you are forest bathing. Though this may sound simple, it will test your focus and concentration. Tuning out everything else around you can make it hard to tune into the sounds of nature. Even when there is no man-made sound, your head is likely full of a cacophony of noise and thoughts. You need to find ways to quiet these thoughts so that you can be one with nature.

1. Start by slowing down. Give yourself some time—it's okay if you can't let go of your thoughts instantly and if you need a bit of practice. Find a spot and sit down in it. Let all of the thoughts in your head come out, and slowly let go of them until you have reached a state of silence.
2. Focus on your breathing. If you are unable to quiet the unwanted thoughts through slowing down, begin breathing deeply. Focus on your breath, and when you breathe out, let go of any distractions.
3. Listen in all directions. If you give it time, the noise in your head will begin to quiet down, and the sounds of nature will fill your mind. Pay attention to what you can hear. Do you hear a bird calling? A woodpecker pecking? Water running through a creek or going down a waterfall? Whatever you hear, try to listen in further and take in the sounds around you.
4. Close your eyes so that you can hear more intensely. Remaining still and quiet and paying attention to the

sounds of the forest around you will help you open your ears and your mind. Be silent, and listen to everything around you. You may hear the trees talking to each other in their phytoncide language when you listen hard enough. Whatever you are hearing, take note of it and appreciate the forest for its beauty (Li, 2019).

* * *

Connecting with Sound

During my walk through the Birks, I sit down by a tree, close my eyes, and let the thoughts in my head melt away. Even though this takes some time, I have learnt to embrace the process and practice my patience. I listen to the trees and what they are saying to each other. I hear the sound of a waterfall in the distance and take in the way I can hear the water coursing over the rocks. I hear the trickling sound of a creek and imagine the life that is living within it. I can hear the leaves rustling in the trees and the sound of a robin singing its beautiful song. Birds communicate with one another, and the flapping of their wings makes me feel as though I can fly high with them. When I tune in to the sounds around me, it feels like anything is possible. All of my stress and anxiety melt away as I listen to nature's music and let it encompass me. I am free—I am whole. I am at one with the earth.

"Listen to the trees as they sway in the wind. Their leaves are telling secrets. Their bark sings songs of olden days as it grows around the trunks. And their roots give names to all things. Their language has been lost. But not the gestures." - Vera Nazarian

* * *

Sight

As humans, we use sight for everything, and all of our interactions with the things and people surrounding us depend on sight. Though sight can be beautiful, most of our time spent seeing is used on screens or urban environments. Though screen time is a certainty of modern life, the huge amount of time we focus on looking at our screen is detrimental to our physical and mental health. Screen time specifically damages the eyes due to blue light - which are very short, high-energy waves produced by LEDs in laptop screens, flat-screen televisions, cell phones, and tablets and are nearly as powerful as UV rays. With the rise of remote working and online schooling, there has been a significant increase in people complaining of headaches, fatigued eyes, and blurred vision—studies have found that one of the most important things to avoid digital eye strain is to establish a screen schedule (Agarwal et al., 2021). Parents have begun to report a higher incidence of ocular problems in their children as online schooling becomes more prevalent. It is essential to take breaks from screen time, especially before sleep, as an overload of screen time will make it more difficult for you to fall asleep and stay asleep. Without taking breaks from screen time, you are causing damage to your eyes that impacts the clarity of your vision and your overall sight health.

Blue light from screens does not only negatively impact our sight health—but it also hurts our mental health. Mood disorders are becoming more and more of an issue, and higher levels of depression and anxiety correlate with the world becoming increasingly digital. Night-time lighting—especially exposure to blue light—harms the circadian rhythm by stopping melatonin production. Disrupted sleep or lack of sleep is a symptom of depression, bipolar disorder, post-traumatic stress disorder, generalized anxiety, and other mood disorders (Dearmont). Lack of sleep, as mentioned in previous chapters, is also linked to various physical issues. A lack of sleep weakens your immune system, making you more susceptible to illness. Though blue light helps you stay awake during the daytime, exposure to it at night-time can harm your sleep cycle. The more time we spend looking at blue light, the more discomfort and strain our eyes experience (Li, 2019). In addition to looking at screens, our eyesight and health are damaged by constantly looking at a cityscape. Living in a city and away from the colours of nature has been proven to make people unhappier and more aggressive due to the grey colours of an urban scene (Li, 2019).

Seeing Fractals

In contrast, colours like blues and greens found in nature have a much more calming effect and can make us less anxious and stressed. Human existence has primarily taken place in nature, even though our modern world continues to move away from natural environments. We are accustomed to nature and reassured by it on a primitive level. When surrounded by green, we feel relaxed and safe, and our instinct tells us that we will not go hungry. The patterns of nature are everywhere, whether in a flower petal, a snowflake, a shell, or anything else (Li, 2019). These patterns bring us calm and help us escape the stress of a digital, urban world. These patterns are known as fractals and can be observed in ocean waves, lightning, coastlines, rivers, flowers, trees, clouds, and snowflakes—they are everywhere around us, and looking at them can reduce stress by as much as 60 percent (Li, 2019). Our mind instinctively responds positively to these patterns.

As humans have evolved, we instinctively respond to nature. It relaxes our eyes and our mind, helping us both mentally and physically. Nature moves in fractals. Nothing in nature is finished—everything is constantly changing and emerging, much like we are in our lives. The fluctuations of our heart look similar to the fluctuations of coastlines, canyons, mountain ranges, or anything else with a pattern (Plevin, 2019). We naturally search for fractal patterns in our surroundings—they bring us great calm and peace and help us de-stress from an increasingly demanding world. Human beings do not respond to urban environments and the hustle and bustle of cities in the same way we respond to nature and the natural world. The chaos of man-made cities is not the same as the chaos of the natural world. Nature is beautiful, endearing, and healthy for our minds and bodies.

> *"There is no better designer than nature."* - Alexander McQueen

Look up

When you are forest bathing, look up. Studies have found that engaging in the simple act of looking up at trees can induce feelings of awe and wonder, which leads to increased feelings of altruism, generosity, and belonging (Plevin, 2019). When you look up into the trees, the sights you take in can result in huge, life-altering changes that help change your perspective on life. Being in awe of nature and realizing the beauty found in the world helps you see things differently. Awe allows us to find new ways of thinking and understanding and change our perspective on the world at large (Plevin, 2019).

When forest bathing you must take steps to appreciate the sights of nature and the fractals surrounding you. This can be done no matter where in nature you are forest bathing—fractals can be found virtually anywhere.

1. Begin by going to a forest, park, garden, or anywhere you can find time to be peaceful.
2. Look up at the clouds and the sky above you. In addition, find other sights of nature to look at—the ripples on the surface of a pond, or the water coming down in a stream, or the way the branches in the tree divide and follow an intricate pattern.
3. Get close up to these sights—look at the veins of a leaf, the petals of a flower, or the pattern of a piece of bark. Notice these patterns and take a mental image in your mind. You will begin to see patterns all around you.
4. Take note of your stress levels before looking at fractals versus your stress levels after looking at fractals. Looking at these patterns can help to significantly reduce your stress levels and help you feel more relaxed and at peace with your surroundings.
5. Once you see how much of the world surrounding you is patterned, you will be able to feel in awe of the natural world, which offers endless beautiful sights. This will

bring you joy, relaxation, and calm—you are a part of these patterns, and you have a beautiful connection with nature that you are finally realizing (Li, 2019).

* * *

Connecting with Sight

I sit in the forest listening to the beautiful sounds of nature. I look around and fully register my surroundings. I am instantly overcome by a sense of calm and euphoria, and I look on, awestruck. The world is a beautiful place, and taking time to forest bathe can open your eyes to this fact and make you see the world, and your life, in a way you never have before. I study everything that I can see from where I am sitting. There are birch trees to one side of me, standing tall and strong, their leaves moving ever so slightly because of the light breeze. They seem to stretch up for eternity, up into the beautiful, clear blue sky above. A leaf falls, landing beside me, and I feel as though this is the tree's way of communicating with me. I offer thanks for this special gift and continue to look all around me.

To another side of me, I see ferns. They are comparably smaller than the birch tree, only stretching for a couple of feet, the highest point they will likely ever get to. Despite their small stature, they are still beautiful and strong. They, too, sway in the wind. Their colour is a vibrant green, which brings me a deep sense of calm and belonging. I can tell that the ferns are communicating with me, too. I take in their messages and feel as though I have found a home here, in this place, at this time. I gently bring my hand up to the fern and brush it against the plant, careful not to bring it any harm. I feel its energy flowing through me, and I take a deep breath.

I see the babbling brook lying not far away. The sounds comfort me, but more than that, the sight of it is beautiful to see. The water courses over the rocks, gently caressing them—one cannot exist without the other. The constant stream of the water helps me understand that life is constantly moving and things are continually changing. I learn to go with the flow, and that, as long as I always take time to be one with nature, I can handle anything life throws at me. I give the brook thanks and let it respond to me. There is always something to be learned from nature, no matter how big or small the message.

I look at the rocks, both around me and sitting in the brook. I reach down and touch one, carefully placing it into my hand and wrapping my fingers around it. I inhale, hold my breath, then slowly exhale. The smoothness of the rock is calming to me, and I can feel the energy it provides coursing through my skin. As I hold this rock, covered in the earth's soil, I look upon the rocks in the water. I see how they change the water stream, how they support it and guide it in the right direction. I feel that this is what nature does for me, too—guides me down the right path, making sure that I am always on track, that I do not go off course. I place the rock back down, and finally, I look at the soil. Some of it has rubbed off on my hand, and I can feel its presence beneath my body. It is the source of everything, and all plants need it to survive. Without the soil, there is no foundation for anything. I thank the soil for supporting all of the beauty that I can see around me, and I feel it is speaking back to me, too. I am one with the Earth. I am at peace. I am free.

"Look! A trickle of water running through some dirt! I'd say our afternoon just got booked solid!" - Bill Watterson

* * *

Smell

Whether we like or hate what we smell, smell gives us a context of our place. When you smell freshly cut grass, you know that it has just been mowed; when you smell trash, you know that it is lying around somewhere nearby. Smelling gives us the ability to know before we see and is the most primal sense we have. No other sense has as direct of an impact on our mind and body as smell does. Smells can significantly affect our mood and how we act; they are connected to memories, both good and bad, and have lasting effects that go far beyond when the smell can no longer be sensed (Li, 2019).

In urban settings, we are often bombarded by smells—many of them unpleasant. Cities do not have the beautiful smell that nature has, as nothing there is really natural. Humans are drawn to the smells of nature, and these scents give us comfort in a way that the smells of the city cannot do. Being in a city constantly diminishes the importance of using our sense of smell, as the smells of a city do not trigger emotional reactions like the smells of nature do.

The Smell of the Forest

Everything in the forest has unique smells. This is especially true for trees. You can recognize the scent of a pine tree, for example, without even seeing it. This is the case for many other types of trees too. A Scots pine tree is one of the most widely distributed conifers in the entire world, and virtually everyone can recognize its scent. It is a strong, dry fragrance, similar to turpentine in some ways; beyond that, the smell of Scots pine can be used "to ease mental and physical fatigue, to clear a cluttered mind and to sharpen focus" (Li, 2019).

A cedar tree also has a beautiful, recognizable scent. Peeling a piece of bark from a cedar tree will reveal a deep, beautiful, and mysterious scent often described as woody, earthy, spicy, and like balsam (Li, 2019). This smell can also be very sweet. Cedar tree essential oils come from the wood itself, whereas the essential oil of many other trees comes from needles and twigs. Cedarwood is often used when making linen chests because the scent of the wood repels moths, fleas, ants, and mosquitoes (Li, 2019). Cedar is great for relaxing and calming oneself, and smelling cedar when you're forest bathing is a great way to de-stress and feel connected with the earth.

The Douglas Fir tree is great for relaxation, and it is said that the essential oil of a Douglas Fir affects the mind and body similar to meditation (Li, 2019). The smell of a Douglas Fir is citrusy, rich, and resinous. It is another tree that you should try to search for when forest bathing. If you are forest bathing to de-stress, the scent of a Douglas Fir is the perfect way to begin your journey.

The scent of a spruce tree is another example of a tree that can help you along your journey of forest bathing. Spruce smells similar to pine but has darker and earthier tones to it. If you are looking to ground yourself while you are forest bathing, look out for a spruce tree—it has a grounding effect. It can encourage a sense of expansiveness, making it perfect for meditation and relaxation during a forest bathing session (Li, 2019).

There are many benefits to using tree essential oils during forest bathing and your everyday life. Depending on the type of tree, essential oils are distilled from the wood or the leaves. If leaves on the trees in your forest fall in winter, this means your forest is deciduous. A deciduous forest has no essential oils but can still be beneficial for its scents, which are often therapeutic (Li, 2019). The steps to creating essential oils go as follows:

1. The oils are first obtained through distillation via steam or water—mechanical methods such as cold pressing may also be used.
2. Once the aromatic chemicals have been extracted, they are combined with a carrier oil to create a ready-for-use product.
3. Essential oils obtained through chemical processes are not considered as being true essential oils.
4. Once made, essential oils are used in practices such as aromatherapy, where they are inhaled through various methods (West, 2019).

There are many benefits to using tree essential oils. Essential oils, aside from being therapeutic, can be used on the skin to relieve aching muscles. The aroma of tree essential oils relaxes and calms the mind and serves to ground oneself. Essential oils can be used in bathwater or diffusers to help keep illnesses away (Li, 2019). Breathing them in can lift your mood and provide you with a burst of energy. Many tree essential oils can also aid sleep for those who struggle with insomnia and other sleep-related disorders. Essential oils can help with headaches and are particularly useful for those who suffer from frequent headaches and migraines. In addition to this, certain tree essential oils contain anti-inflammatory properties and can be used to reduce allergic airway inflammation; they can be also be used as antimicrobial and anticancer agents (Rashan et al., 2019).

The Smell of the Earth

The smell of the forest holds various health benefits and breathing in the air of the forest has been found to calm the nervous system. Various smells of the earth can be found in the forest, especially the smell of soil and rain along with particular trees. The soil microbe *M. vaccae* has a smell itself—this smell is known as geosmin, and it is the dirt smell that provides foods such as beetroots and carrots with an earthy taste (Li, 2019). Many foods have the smell of the earth—you can even taste a region's microbes in things such as wine, cheese, and chocolate. Humans are sensitive to geosmin—we can even detect it at levels as low as five parts per trillion. This chemical allowed us to find food in our foraging days (Li, 2019). Our primal instincts draw us to the smell of geosmin, and we are naturally calmed when we inhale the scent. The smell of soil and rain is instantly recognizable because of the microbes that create geosmin.

Part of the reason we are drawn to nature and forests is because of the smell. However, there are things in the forest air that we can't smell that still contribute to our happiness when we are in nature—negative air ions. Negative ions have positive, energizing effects on us. They can improve our mental clarity and make us happier overall. Negative ions are primarily found in nature instead of indoors and are abundant around waterfalls, rivers, and streams (Li, 2019). Breathing in negative ions goes down the path of our nervous system, allowing us to feel a sense of calm and peace within the forest—practising meditative breathing when you are forest bathing and taking in negative ions along with the smells of nature surrounding you is key to improving your forest bathing experience. The smells of the forest bring us great comfort and euphoria, more so than scents from indoor environments do.

The Power of Breathing

Yogic breathing is a great thing to practice when you are forest bathing. Yogic breathing gives us a feeling of calm and helps us to connect with our surroundings. Some of the most popular forms of yogic breathing include:

- Ocean breath, or *Ujjayi*. This is used in support of yoga postures and involves constricting the back of your throat to support lengthening for every breath cycle you do. It concentrates and directs the breath, allowing extra power and focus, along with increasing oxygen consumption (Pizer, 2020).
- Breath of Fire, or *Kapalabhati*. This method of yogic breathing involves normal inhalations and powerful, fast exhalations. Forced exhalation can reduce stress, boost and improve brain function, and improve respiratory health. It strengthens the abdominal muscles and improves digestion (Nunez, 2020).
- Solar breath, or *Surya Bhedana*. This practice involves using the right nostril to breathe in and the left nostril to

breathe out. Breathing in through the right nostril affects alternative energies that exist within our body. It activates body functions, improves digestion, clears your sinuses, and warms the body. It is the best breathing exercise for anyone suffering from a cold as well (Singh, 2021).
- Lunar breath, or *Chandra Bhedana*. This is similar to solar breath, but in this case, the left nostril is used for inhalation while the right nostril is used for exhalation (Singh, 2021).

Once you have decided on the suitable form of yogic breathing for you, you can begin to follow the steps to put yogic breathing into practice.

1. Try mountain pose to begin. Breathe in with your preferred yogic method, and as you inhale, raise your arms above your head.
2. Hold the pose for a count of four.
3. Reach higher, raising yourself onto your toes, then rotating your hands to face outward.
4. Begin breathing out while you lower your arms.
5. Get into the starting position again, filling your lungs with the fresh air of the forest.
6. Repeat three times (Li, 2019).

* * *

Connecting with Smell

As I continue along the trail, I find a cute little bench looking out into the valley. I sit on the bench, admiring the view and trying to take in everything around me. I recognize all the smells surrounding me—the damp soil on the ground, earthy and inviting. The trees and the plants, and their unique scents, each different and enticing. The fresh air, crisp, enters my lungs as I begin to breathe—the smell of the waterfall not far from me now. I let the sound vibrate in my ears and imagine what it must look like based on what I am smelling. Perhaps I reach out to touch something, grounding myself both through touch and through smell. I am here, and I am present.

I utilize some of my favourite yogic breathing techniques. Depending on the day, I may switch up which technique I use—I often switch every forest bathing session to get all of the benefits of each type of yogic breathing. As I breathe, I enter my yoga pose if I have decided to do one for the day. Though the practice is called yogic breathing, it's not necessarily vital that you physically do yoga while you are breathing. Yogic breathing is a practice in and of itself, and it doesn't need another component added to it if you do not wish to. Breathing in and out is often enough for me and allows me to smell the earth around me, giving me a deep sense of calm. I feel that I am home, that I belong here. The smells of the earth have become like the smell of home to me now that I regularly practice forest bathing, and breathing in the scents makes me feel like a warm blanket is being wrapped around me. I feel a level of comfort that I can't get anywhere else, and I thank the Earth for all of the beautiful things it has to offer to me.

"Nature has been for me, for as long as I remember, a source of solace, inspiration, adventure, and delight; a home, a teacher, a companion." - Lorraine Anderson.

* * *

Touch

Out of all five senses, touch is the most gentle and intimate one. It allows us to communicate without words and is the best form of non-verbal communication that we have at our disposal. We use touch to tell people how we feel, making it essential to all of our relationships. Though we use touch for communication, we also use it for virtually everything else. There are plenty of things we touch on a day-to-day basis. We touch our clothes and our shoes when we are getting dressed for the day, our car keys when we are ready to go, our cup of coffee when we are up in the morning, the doorknob of our apartment building or office—we touch more things that we can count daily.

Though touch connects us with our surroundings, the things we touch on a day-to-day basis often disconnect us from nature. The majority of what we are touching is man-made objects instead of things found in the natural world. Because of this, it can be difficult to ground ourselves in the world around us through touch. "It is with our sense of touch that we can begin to physically reconnect with nature…many of our illnesses, stresses and anxieties are due to a lack of connection with nature" (Li, 2019).

The man-made objects that we are constantly touching only serve to take us further away from nature. With every object we touch, we are pulled further into an artificial world, one that is suffering from a severe disconnect to what is natural. The clicking of our fingers against the keyboard as we type serves only as a way of pulling us further into a digital landscape and away from nature. At the end of a long day, everything that we have touched has, in some way, furthered our disconnect from nature and the earth surrounding us. We live in apartment blocks surrounded by concrete, the noise of other people, and whatever we touch in our home is man-made, too. It's virtually impossible to escape touching man-made objects, especially when the population moves towards living in urban environments.

Grounding Yourself in Nature

You must remember to ground yourself in nature through touch. Touch can be a beautiful, important sense at our disposal, but it is often not used correctly. When you are practising forest bathing, you should take the time to focus on touching what is around you and on connecting with the earth through touch.

To ground yourself in nature, begin by taking your shoes off. Going barefoot when you are forest bathing is an amazingly simple way of connecting yourself with the earth, and this simple touch can ground you in nature. Our feet connect us to the world—they are a physical link between us and the earth that supports our bodies. When you walk barefoot in nature, you create an electrical circuit that allows you to recharge and revive through nature. When we bring our feet in contact with the earth's electrical charge, we receive powerful restorative electrons that the earth offers to every living thing—the earth is like a giant battery in this way (Li, 2019). Because the earth is essentially a power source, it is the perfect way to recharge when we are drained from the tasks of life. Forest bathing should be all about recharging and reconnecting. It can act as an energy source for you and calm your nerves when your stress is too high. The natural recharging power that the earth offers will flow through your body when your feet hit the ground.

Many people may not realize how vital feet are to our health. Pressure points on our feet hold incredible restorative powers, and focusing on our feet when we are forest bathing holds similar recharging powers. Foot reflexology is a practice that has been around for centuries, and that involves focusing on different pressure points in our feet to gain certain health benefits. Studies have found that foot reflexology may help with stress and relaxation, digestion, eye strain, and improved sleep; in addition, it is naturally soothing and relaxing to those practising it (Quinn, 2021). Utilizing your feet and pressure points in forest bathing can therefore contribute to the level of relaxation you feel during your journey. If you decide that you want to go barefoot during your forest bathing experience, you should take some simple steps in grounding exercises to make sure that you are doing it the right way.

1. Take off your socks and shoes, and then go outside.
2. Stand on the earth, grass, or sand—wherever you have decided to practice forest bathing.
3. Stand with both feet on the ground so you can have two points of contact to form an electrical circuit. If you are lying down, make a circuit with one foot and one elbow.
4. Stay grounded for twenty minutes every day.
5. Avoid glass, and don't stand on anything that has been sprayed with pesticides.
6. If you want to take this further, you can continue to ground yourself by sitting or standing and focusing all of your attention on the soles of your feet. Pay attention to

what you can feel during this.
7. Stand with your feet parallel and shoulder-width apart. While doing this, keep your chin tucked in and your spine straight. Let your arms hang loose at your sides, and let all of your tension and weight sink into your feet. Picture roots spreading out from the bottom of your feet and going into the earth beneath you—this is a great way to feel the electrical current you are creating by going barefoot (Li, 2019).

Though going barefoot is an amazing way to restore the broken connection between you and the natural world, there are other methods you can use while you are forest bathing. Touch does not only have to be done by going barefoot—touching anything in nature around you can help to ground you and connect you to the beauty and natural restorative powers of nature.

One of the many ways to use touch when forest bathing is by running your hands through leaves. Pay attention to the different textures that you feel, and allow the leaves' energy to course through you. Feel the life that is pulsing below the surface of these leaves and how the earth is providing the leaves with life in the same way it is providing you with life. Connecting yourself physically to leaves is a great way to feel the forest's energy. You can also utilize touch by touching the water in a stream or waterfall and letting it run over your hands. Connecting with water is another great way to ground yourself when you are forest bathing and remind yourself that you are one with the earth. As the water flows over your hand, think of all of the life it has seen—it has been here for ages and will continue to live on in this forest, providing life and shelter to various creatures. Thank the water for everything that it does for all living things.

You can also try connecting with touch by picking up and feeling the surface of rocks. Pay attention to how the textures are similar or different—is the rock smooth or bumpy and coarse? Does it chip off in a cloud of fine dust, or is it sturdy and unbreakable? Whatever the case, give thanks to the rocks for being a part of the forest. In their own way, rocks are also providing you with the energy you are looking to gain from your forest bathing experience. Even if you don't realize it, rocks are full of energy, and touching them can give you that burst of energy that you are searching for.

* * *

Connecting with Touch

When I forest bathe, I make it a point to touch everything around me. This gives me the chance to connect to the surrounding world in a way that I am not typically granted. It makes me feel rejuvenated and alive and is one of the best sensations of touch that I can experience when forest bathing. Paying attention to the pressure points in my feet helps me de-stress, and the soil marking my skin only relaxes me further. However, this is not the only form of touch that I use when I am forest bathing. I make sure that I utilize my hands too, as they are the primary tool we use to experience touch in our everyday lives.

I begin by taking off my shoes by the babbling brook which runs through the Birks of Aberfeldy. There is a light breeze, and I feel how it caresses my skin like a gentle hand. I inhale the fresh air, and I bring my feet down onto the ground. Instantly, I am struck with a feeling of connection and wholeness. I can feel the electricity as it courses through my body, and I cherish this valuable moment. I let the electricity run through me for a minute, breathing in and breathing out the whole time. As I edge closer to the water, I begin to feel its coolness beneath my feet. The water flows over my feet, encompassing them, and I close my eyes to bask in the power of its energy.

I think of how life cannot exist without water and how it powers everything around us. My body is composed of almost entirely water, and I can feel my connection with it as I stand in the brook. I reach down, grasping at the stones. The ones below my feet are covered in a furry moss, soft and welcoming. The ones lying in my hands are smooth, sturdy, and cool to the touch. I can feel all of the energy flowing into my body, and I continue to breathe, in and out, in and out. I begin to feel the power of my existence, and I slowly recharge as I connect myself with the earth. I grasp onto the rock in my hand tightly, unwilling to let it go. It's a connection like I've never felt before.

"Climb the mountains and get their good tidings. Nature's peace will flow into you as sunshine flows into trees. The winds will blow their own freshness into you, and the storms their energy, while cares will drop away from you like the leaves of Autumn." - John Muir

* * *

Taste

Taste is the final of our five senses. Regularly, humans eat and drink unhealthy foods that can have negative impacts on our health. We live in a society where healthy foods are considered boring and unappetizing, whereas unhealthy foods are considered tasty and fun. Though indulging in junk food now and then isn't bad, people tend to overeat junk food. This can cause a large number of health problems. One of the most prevalent health problems this leads to is obesity. In the United States, the proportion of the adult population considered obese grew from 13.95 percent in 1976-1980 to 29.57 percent by 1999-2000, substantially higher than European countries with the highest obesity rates (Tomer, 2011). Rises in obesity rates are occurring in nearly all developed and developing countries.

Aside from causing obesity, overeating junk food can lead to mental health issues such as depression. Studies have found that, compared to midlife women with very little or no depression symptoms, midlife women who reported depression symptoms reported eating fast food regularly (Lee and Allen, 2021). Young adults specifically are most likely to consume unhealthy foods over healthy foods; this leads to higher rates of depression and mental illness in adolescents. In contrast, young adults who consume more healthy foods than unhealthy foods have decreased depression and mental illness risk. Poor nutrition can lead to a slew of other health problems. According to the Centre for Disease Control (CDC), poor nutrition has been linked to heart disease and stroke, type two diabetes, cancer, and deficits in brain function.

Processed foods typically include various artificial flavours, and elaborate ingredients are generally considered more unhealthy than unprocessed foods. Processed foods have likely contributed to the obesity epidemic and chronic diseases from poor nutrition. Processed foods are high in sugar and fats, making them dangerous to consume in high volumes (CDC, 2021).

There are numerous benefits to eating healthy, natural food. Without processing, food is lower in sugars and fats that can cause chronic diseases. Natural foods are loaded with important nutrients that keep you healthy. They are also better for the environment and can be a great way to connect to the earth. Natural foods help you manage your blood pressure and are good for your skin. They nourish and protect you. Many natural and unprocessed foods are high in healthy fats and can reduce the risk of serious disease. Many are also full of antioxidants vital to your health and can help you lead a better life.

Foraging Wild Foods

When you are forest bathing, you should consider foraging and eating wild foods. Be careful when you are doing this—eating wild foods can be dangerous if you do not know what you are doing. Be sure only to eat foods you are familiar with. When you find something safe to eat, you can use foraging as another way to connect with nature. Foraging for food in the forest will allow you to taste the beautiful nature around you and can be a great way to fully immerse yourself in the forest bathing experience.

We are made to interact with nature. It is in our blood, in our history. It is our primal instinct. When you see food during your journey forest bathing, your instincts will tell you to forage it. For most of our history, people have foraged their food—for a long time, foraging was the only way to stay alive and fed. Not foraging food is a relatively new practice in the timeline of human history. Human development "depends on the integration of slow life history, complex production skills, and extensive sociality…humans are distinguished by a suite of life history traits" (Koster et al., 2020). Foraging is included in these traits. Just as our ancestors foraged for their food, we should continue to forage for ours when we connect with nature.

It is important to remember that just because something is edible for animals, this does not mean it will be edible for humans. However, there are many common foods that people have foraged for centuries. These foods can not only be found in stores—but they can also be found in most parts of the world. For example, a prickly pear cactus can be found in most deserts in the world. Provided that you remove the spines and peel the cactus correctly, you can enjoy a delicious juice. Dandelions are also completely edible, a fact that few people know. Though they might seem like a mere annoyance in your yard, dandelions are safe to eat and can be foraged virtually anywhere. Blackberries and other forms of berries are easily recognisable and can be a great thing to forage. This is one of the most common foods that can be foraged during your forest bathing journey. Chickweed is easy to identify if you know what you are looking for and grows in yards, grasslands, forests, and roadsides. Pine nuts are another great food to forage for—if you have the patience and experience. Seek pine trees with large seeds to make the process of extracting them easier ("Foraging for Beginners," 2017).

Drinking water from forest streams is another way to taste the forest bathing experience. Though you should keep in mind that drinking from unknown water sources can be dangerous, drinking from running water and using a filtered water bottle can help you connect with the earth.

Bringing your own food

When forest bathing, prepare healthy, natural snacks to bring with you. One recipe that you should consider trying is chocolate oat bran muffins, an original recipe by Aly Michell in 2020. These muffins are plant-based, gluten-free, and primarily made with oat bran or old-fashioned oats. They are full of fibre and can also be altered to be sugar-free.

To make these muffins, you will need eight ingredients:

- one cup oat bran,
- ⅓ cup cocoa powder,
- ¼ cup sugar or date paste,
- 1 teaspoon baking powder,
- ¼ teaspoon salt,
- ½ cup vegan milk,
- 1 banana, and
- ¼ cup chocolate chips (if you choose to add them).

The recipe goes as follows:

1. Preheat your oven to 450 degrees Fahrenheit (Around 230 degrees Celsius). Grease a six-mould muffin or cupcake tin, or use cupcake liners.
2. Combine oat bran, cocoa powder, sugar, baking powder, and salt in a bowl. Add sugar if you are using it.
3. If you are replacing sugar with date paste, blend the paste with milk and banana.
4. Combine all of the ingredients.
5. Pour the batter into the prepared tin, and top with chocolate chips if you would like to. Bake for 15-17 minutes, and then let cool for 15 minutes.
6. Drizzle natural peanut butter or add a jam to the top of the muffin. You can also use your favourite vegan butter.

* * *

Connecting with Taste

When I go on my forest bathing trips, I bring a healthy snack with me. I sit down in the forest and unpack my bag, taking out the food I prepared the night before. I typically bring a sandwich filled with plant-based ingredients to feel connected to everything the natural world offers. I take a bite. The taste of vegetables and plants connects me to everything that is surrounding me. Once I finish eating my sandwich, I take my filtered water bottle out of my bag. I go by the stream and fill it up until it reaches the top. I take a long, cool sip of the water. I don't know if it tastes any different from other water in reality, but it feels unique to me. The taste hits my tongue, and I take in the beauty of what the world has to offer. Whenever I am thirsty, I return to the stream and fill up my bottle once again. It doesn't matter how different this water is from any other water—to me, it is the freshest and most amazing thing I have ever tasted.

"Live in each season as it passes; breathe the air, drink the drink, taste the fruit, and resign yourself to the influence of the earth." - Henry David Thoreau

The Sixth Sense

Plenty of people believe that we have more than five senses. The sixth sense connects us with the world on a more spiritual level. This sense "is what we feel in nature that can be so hard to describe—a feeling of wonder and excitement, transcendence and even ecstasy" (Li, 2019). It's hard to pinpoint exactly what this sense is—regardless of what to call it, it is there, and we feel more connected with nature when experiencing this sixth sense. Nature can provide us with happiness that we cannot get anywhere else in the world. When you feel your sixth sense activated, you see the world through a different lens and experience euphoria.

Sitting in a sacred spot encourages your sixth sense. This sacred spot can be anywhere that feels special to you—a spot where you feel fully and truly connected with nature. This could be your yard, a park, a garden, or a specific area of the forest. Let yourself be still in this space, and make it sacred yourself. Enter this sacred space with reverence, and give it offerings and loving energy; consider cleaning it as you would your own home (Plevin, 2019). You can name this place and begin to develop your own special relationship with it.

Another way to connect with your sixth sense is by simply letting go. Try to figure out what is troubling you and what is holding you back. Put a name to whatever you want to manifest. Pick up a stick or a fallen leaf that you find in the forest, and think of something that you are worried or anxious over—then drop it. Let it go as you would let go of anything else. Lie down on the earth, and allow your body to sink into the ground while the earth holds you. You will truly connect with your sixth sense when you do this, bringing you unimaginable peace (Plevin, 2019).

Close your eyes, and listen to your intuition to guide you—do you want to walk in a specific direction or sit down in a place that feels like home to you? Connect with all of your senses that you can feel in the forest. Ask yourself how everything you are feeling and experiencing makes you react emotionally. Let time drop away, and let go of all of your worldly worries—in this moment, when you are truly connected with your sixth sense, these things do not matter (Li, 2019).

* * *

Connecting with my Sixth Sense

In the Birks of Aberfeldy, I engage with my sixth sense. Once I have finished my food and water break, I begin by closing my eyes and looking inward. I ask myself what I am feeling and analyse all of the thoughts coursing through my mind. It is difficult at first—I am resisting letting go, that I am so used to holding on to my worries that I have forgotten what it is to have none. Though I doubt that I will be able to let go, I find that I can begin looking inward once I give it time. I reflect on my forest bathing experience so far, understanding how I have truly connected to the world around me and lost myself in nature. I let my instincts decide where I will go next, if there is a specific direction I am drawn to, or if I am content where I am. Wherever I end up, I feel the happiness that comes with the sixth sense. The sixth sense is about letting go—it is about forgetting your worldly worries and finding your truest sense of happiness in nature.

> "Should you shield the canyons from the wind storms you would never see the true beauty of their carvings."
> - Elisabeth Kübler-Ross

Let Nature Guide You

Self-Love

Self-love is crucial to having a successful forest bathing experience. Before we can give our love to the earth, we must first give love to ourselves. As humans, we are notoriously hard on ourselves. We are our own worst critics most of the time. We have been taught our whole lives that what we have to offer is not enough, and because of this, we struggle to be satisfied with who we are. When you love yourself, you can change the world. It is essential to thank your body for everything that it does—it protects you and blesses you and should be treated as precious (Plevin, 2019). When we can see the beauty of nature, we can notice the beauty that we hold, too. By being able to love ourselves, we can begin to love others and the earth.

Ecotherapy is an incredible practice that helps you love yourself and nature. Researchers at the University of Essex found that, among people suffering from depression, 90 percent had a higher level of self-esteem after they walked through a park, and nearly 75 percent reported feeling less depressed (Plevin, 2019). People suffering from mental illness largely reported that contact with nature helped them to cope with their feelings. Ecotherapy can promote better mental health. Ecotherapy holds the belief that restoration can take place in the context of the relationship between humans and nature (Sackett, 2010). Ecotherapy helps to take people away from the digital world we live in and is the most natural form of therapy available to us.

When you connect with nature, you can learn to accept yourself for who you truly are—the good and the bad. Let nature guide you along your journey of self-discovery. While forest bathing, you will be filled with internal voices and emotions. Take note of these, and let yourself think about whatever floats into your mind. You may not always agree with your internal voice, but it is important to respect it as you would anyone else's opinion. Give your internal voice and your emotions space to say what they have to say—in the end, it will help you to improve yourself and, most importantly, to love yourself more.

> "The earth has its music for those who will listen." - George Santayana

Following the Signs

Begin forest bathing by taking in nature's signs. You can do this in a figurative or literal way. Follow the path that nature is guiding you on and that your internal voice is calling you to go down. If there are no physical signs or guideposts where you are forest bathing, listen to your instinct—it will take you to where you need to be. You can also follow physical signs and guideposts if the area you are forest bathing in has them. The signs are there for a reason: to show you your path and direct you to where you need to be. When you are walking through the woods and come across a signpost, you can use this to confirm that you are on the path you are meant to be on. These signposts can also allow you to see that you can take any path that you wish—sometimes there will be signs pointing in different directions, and you will have to decide where to go, much like you would in real life.

Similar to a signpost, a guidepost points you the way that you should be going. A guidepost doesn't have to be the same as a literal signpost—it can manifest in different forms, such as a person telling you to take a certain path or a tree blocking your typical route (Plevin, 2019). What may seem like a barrier can actually be a blessing. By asking the universe for guidance on which path to take, you will be given the help you need. If you are ever unsure of where to go when you are forest bathing, trust that the universe will give you the messages you need to hear to make the right decision.

Using signposts and guideposts can help you to listen to the teachings of nature. Nature itself acts as a metaphor—there is a deeper meaning to everything that can be found in nature, even if we are unaware of what that meaning is. As you spend more time forest bathing, you will learn to understand what nature is trying to say to you (Plevin, 2019). Open yourself up to the possibilities and be willing to listen to the natural world. Nature wants to support you along your journey as a human being. People are always evolving, discovering new things, and changing as people, so connecting with nature is an important way to foster our self-development. You are always in the process of becoming the person that you are meant to be. Just as you enter the forest with your intentions, nature has intentions for you. If you are called to a certain object that you find in the forest, open yourself up to listening.

Finding a Sacred Object

Huaca, a Quechuan word for "sacred object," is critical to the emotional journey you take while forest bathing. A *Huaca* can help ground you. Pay attention to the objects around you when you are on your trip. When you find something particularly intriguing, simply ask: "Are you my *Huaca?*" If you receive a yes, you know that you have found your sacred object (Plevin, 2019). Your sacred object should be something you can take home that will remind you of your special, sacred place. Remember to ask permission from nature first and ask this of the object itself. The first object you find may not be your sacred object—don't be discouraged if this is the case. Try to connect with every object that catches your eye. See what emotions are brought forth by the object of your choosing. When something is your sacred object, you will know in your heart that you have found it.

Finding Your Own Way

Forest bathing is different for everyone. There is no one way to do forest bathing correctly. When you are forest bathing, you can find your way and purpose in life and nature. The more you practice forest bathing, the more accustomed you will become to it. You need to discover your relationship with nature and how it applies to and impacts your life. Like how plants offer their own medicine and have a purpose and a role in nature, we as human beings have a purpose for being on Earth. We, too, offer medicine that acts as a form of restoration that is needed (Plevin, 2019). The medicine of nature, and the medicine that you create yourself, can be given to other people, or it can be used to help you. Your medicine always has a greater purpose and meaning—it is up to you to figure out what that meaning is.

Finding your way with forest bathing may take time. It's important not to be discouraged if this is the case. The first time you forest bathe, you may not know exactly which direction to take. Maybe you fear that you aren't doing it right or don't have what it takes to connect with nature. Know that these are just thoughts and not facts. These things take their time to reveal themselves to you, and the purpose of forest bathing in your life may take time to reveal itself, too.

Listen to nature, and build a strong connection with it. Once you have opened yourself up, you will find that nature is more than willing to communicate with you—in fact, nature wants to help you along your journey as much as possible. Be open, and be mindful. The more you practice forest bathing, the easier it will become for you, and the messages you receive from nature will only be amplified over time.

> *"Of all the paths you take in life, make sure a few of them are dirt." - John Muir*

How to End Your Forest Bath

Ending your forest bath on a good note is just as important as beginning it on a good note. On your way into the forest, you expressed your gratitude for everything it had to offer you. You must repeat this action as you prepare to leave. After giving offerings during your journey, it is time to offer one final thanks to the forest for everything it has taught you and for the progress it has allowed you to make.

Thank the Forest

Thank the forest for keeping you protected, for sharing its powers, for all of the knowledge and wisdom you gained, and for the space you were given to discover yourself (Plevin, 2019). Thank the forest for showing up, for enduring through difficult times, for being resilient and a fighter, and for standing tall and strong (Plevin, 2019). Thank everything surrounding you in nature, from the animals to the soil to the streams and the trees. Let yourself be filled with overwhelming gratitude for everything you have gained on your journey and your lessons. As humans, we are accustomed to complaining about what is wrong in our life. It is natural to focus on the negative because that is what we have been taught to do. It is much rarer to focus on the positive. Take this opportunity to thank the forest for allowing you to see the good in life and all of the world's beauty.

Practice this same type of gratitude as you journey throughout life. We often don't realize how beautiful life actually is. When you feel negative, think of things you are thankful for and make you happy. Keep a mental list of these things so that you can return to them whenever you are sad or stressed. Practice gratitude every single day, regardless of whether you are forest bathing that day. By doing this, "you may find that the sun shines brighter, colours are more vivid, smells are more divine, and the world is more full of joy" (Plevin, 2019). Journal about the things that bring you joy and about the lessons that the forest has taught you.

Time for Reflection

It is time for you to reflect on your journey. As you head back over the threshold, make a mental or physical note of what you gained and learned from the day. Think of what nature gave you during this time and of your gratefulness for all of its gifts. If this takes some time, that is okay—give yourself as much time and space as you need to recognize everything you have just learned and experienced fully. If you received important messages during your time forest bathing, note these for future reference. During difficult times, coming back to these messages can give you a positive outlook on life once again.

If you're practising forest bathing with others, take the time to share your reflections. Because everyone has such different experiences with forest bathing, it can be eye-opening to hear what others gain. Form a circle, use a talking piece, and give everyone a chance to share their story and their reflection—it will inspire and amaze you more than you realize (Plevin, 2019). Sharing with others can help you to understand your own experience on a deeper level as well. There are numerous benefits of self-reflection. It not only expands your mind but strengthens who you are as a person and helps you to become the best version of yourself. Open yourself up to the world, and you will learn more about yourself than you ever imagined was possible.

Maintaining the Connection

Applying the lessons you learn during forest bathing to your daily life involves incorporating simple, doable things you have gained through your journey. As you navigate through your day-to-day life, learn to give gratitude to everything you do. There are plenty of times throughout the day to express gratitude for nature and the Earth. You will not be in nature all of the time, but this does not mean that you cannot still connect with nature on a deep and meaningful level. Doing something as simple as brushing your teeth can be used as a chance to thank the Earth for the water that you need to complete the activity. Sipping water and eating foods from nature is another opportunity to reflect on the water and food that the world provides for you. Consider praying to the water that comes out of your tap the same way that you prayed to and gave thanks to the stream in the forest (Plevin, 2019). Bringing the beauty of nature into your everyday life will help you maintain the happiness and peace that you gained during forest bathing.

Stay mindful and present in your everyday life after your forest bathing experience. One way to continue practising mindfulness daily is to keep objects collected while forest bathing with you and placing them around your home, work desk, car, or anywhere removed from nature. When you begin to feel stressed or anxious, take time to find a connection to nature and the universe. This can be done by using essential oils, lighting a candle, watering a plant, or looking at pictures of nature (Plevin, 2019). Stay in touch with your senses, and continue to notice all of them the same way you did in nature. Keep track of all of the natural things you can sense, such as the taste and feel of water, the smell of essential oils, or the sight of trees outside your window. Activate your sixth sense by bringing yourself back to the memories of your forest bath.

* * *

Wandering and Reflecting

As my forest bathing journey continues, I wander through the woods. I let my feet take me wherever nature is guiding me to go, paying attention to any signposts or guideposts that I notice. I keep my mind open and aware and take note of subtle signs that I see along the path. I pass fallen branches and let them act as a guide telling me which direction I should be taking. I come across a puddle in the ground and look at how the sun reflects off the water, making it shine like diamonds. I take this puddle as a blessing and consider it a sign telling me which way to go—it would be difficult to get around it, so I believe that this is nature telling me to go the other way. I find a stream as I continue to walk and follow the direction of the water. I listen to what nature has to tell me and follow its instructions.

As I continue walking, I listen to the forest while being as open and mindful as I can be. Though I am relaxed, stressful thoughts and distractions about work begin to jump into my mind. Despite them being unwanted, I choose not to suppress them—nature has taught me that I should acknowledge and see everything that comes into my head and take the necessary steps to let it go. Even if this does not work every time, my intention is there, and I know that I am doing my best to focus on the here and now. As I reach the end of the trail and the end of my journey, I make my way back to the car park. Before I leave the canopy of trees, I place my hand on a nearby birch tree and feel its bark underneath my palm, beautiful and coarse. I use all of the senses at my disposal to take this tree in and memorize the forest's beauty. As I rest my hand on the tree, I thank the forest for guiding and protecting me throughout my journey and teaching me things I could not have learned on my own.

Though it was difficult for me to fully disconnect from work and normal life at times, I still feel I have accomplished something great. My ability to reconnect with nature was a success, and I feel much calmer and less stressed out than I did before my journey. Even if I could not let everything in the world go, I let enough go to enjoy my time and learn from nature. I will take these lessons back into my everyday life and show my gratitude for nature every day.

"When you do something noble and beautiful and nobody noticed, do not be sad. For the sun every morning is a beautiful spectacle and yet most of the audience still sleeps."
- John Lennon

* * *

Growing your own Forest

Fill Your House with Plants

Even if you wanted to, it is impossible to forest bathe all of the time. However, there are ways that you can adopt forest bathing at home and work that will help make the transition from nature to everyday life easier. One of the simplest ways to do this is to begin filling your house with plants. Plants help us breathe—when we breathe in, we bring in oxygen, and when we breathe out, we release carbon dioxide. Plants do the opposite—our relationship is symbiotic, and we rely upon one another for our survival. Having more oxygen in our home is good for us because oxygen affects every part of our body. Plants can also purify the air, as indoor air can be two to five times more polluted than outdoor air (Li, 2019). According to NASA, some of the best air-purifying plants include:

- Peace lily
- Golden pothos
- English ivy
- Chrysanthemum
- Gerbera daisy

- Mother-in-law's tongue
- Bamboo palm
- Azalea
- Red-edge dracaena
- Spider plant

The Smell of Nature Inside

Natural essential oils have unique benefits that can help you transition from nature to indoors. Some of the best essential oils to bring the smell of nature into your home include eucalyptus, which can be used as a topical pain reliever and decongestant and will bring the smell of the plant into your home. Other plant-based essential oils can be used throughout your home, too, such as lavender, which is good if you are looking for a calming, sleep-inducing oil. Frankincense can bring the smell of nature into your home as well and acts as a mood-enhancer and stress-reducer, similar to nature. Chamomile essential oil can help you regenerate from colds, fevers, and nausea and will also provide you with a relaxing effect in the same way that nature can (Slater, 2018). When you are using essential oils, you should also consider taking advantage of diffusers and reed diffusers. Diffusers can be used as an alternative to candles and incense, as you don't breathe in any smoke and the oils remain in their original form. Filling a diffuser with some water and a few drops of essential oil will give your home the scent of nature and will stay in the air for several hours (Li, 2019).

Candles can be another great way of bringing nature into your home. Candles come in various natural scents that resemble the smells of nature, and you can purchase candles scented like various plants and trees. Watching the flame of a candle is a way to connect yourself to the natural world and can be a therapeutic and meditative practice. If you want to smell nature in your home, you should keep wood shavings and potpourri around. This will fill your home with the smell of nature, ensuring that you don't feel far removed from the natural world every time you are there. This smell can help ground you and keep you present, which is important when experiencing high stress levels.

"Smell is a potent wizard that transports you across thousands of miles and all the years you have lived. The odours of fruits waft me to my southern home, to my childhood frolics in the peach orchard. Other odours, instantaneous and fleeting, cause my heart to dilate joyously or contract with remembered grief. Even as I think of smells, my nose is full of scents that start to awake sweet memories of summers gone and ripening fields far away." - Hellen Keller

Drinking Herbal Teas

Different types of herbal teas can help you connect with nature through your senses of smell and taste and help you be healthier overall.

Eucalyptus tea brings you back to the forest and plants' smell and gives you a way to taste nature. In addition to this, however, eucalyptus tea can help support your respiratory system, reduce inflammation and lower blood sugar, and has antibacterial properties. ("Health Benefits of Herbal Teas," 2020).

Rosemary tea brings the smell of the natural herb into your home and serves as a great reminder of the scents of the forest. Besides being a delicious herb to use in your food, rosemary tea can help reduce inflammation, and improve digestion ("Health Benefits of Herbal Teas," 2020).

Ginger tea also recalls the smells of nature while including benefits such as aiding digestion, reducing heartburn and inflammation, improving blood circulation, and supporting the immune system ("Health Benefits of Herbal Teas," 2020).

While not a herbal tea, Green tea can also boost and benefit your health and bring you back to the feeling of forest bathing. Green tea can help improve your brain function, and boost your metabolism and immune system ("Health Benefits of Herbal Teas," 2020).

Set Your Body to Forest Time

According to the circadian rhythm, humans are meant to wake up at first light and fall asleep when it becomes dark. Originally, humans took in only natural light, keeping our circadian clocks balanced. However, people are now more likely to be exposed to light after it gets dark outside. When this happens, our bodies remain in daytime mode—our heart rate goes up, our brains are still active, and our production of melatonin is suppressed (Li, 2019). Technology has thrown us off of the circadian rhythm. Many people work in front of screens all day, and when it gets dark, they partake in leisure activities in front of a screen. The blue light from our screens interferes with our circadian rhythm, which ultimately negatively impacts our health. Artificial lights have resulted in a loss of the evening reduction in light that typically gives our bodies the cue that it is time to sleep (Dong et al., 2019).

There are some ways to reset your body to forest time that will better reflect our circadian rhythm. The first thing you should do to be on forest time is remove blue light. Though removing technology may seem like the simplest way to do this, lighting alternatives can be used, such as smart lighting or having a circadian light. Green exercises (exercising outdoors) during the day can also be beneficial to fixing your circadian cycle. There is evidence to suggest that exercise is easier when you are doing it in nature and that people tend to walk faster outdoors than they do indoors (Gladwell et al., 2013).

Along with decreasing the risk for depression and other mental illnesses, exercising in green space can improve your physical body and make you more inclined to exercise intensively. Green exercise improves self-esteem and negative moods such as tension, anger, and depression; there is an immediate psychological benefit to exercising in nature (Gladwell et al., 2013). There are many types of green exercises that you can do, ranging from a walk or gentle yoga to running, hiking, or climbing.

Going on forest bathing breaks and holidays is another great way to set yourself to forest time. Spending several nights in the forest and away from technology exposes you to natural light, putting your body on a schedule that allows you to feel restored and reset. When you fix your circadian rhythm, you will find that you are happier and feel healthier.

Forest Bathing at Work

Given that we spend so much of our time at work, it can be hard to find time to forest bathe. Even if you want to practice forest bathing regularly, the demands of work make this impossible. However, there are small ways that you can practice forest bathing while you are at work. A simple way to do this is to have office plants. If you have your own space at work, plants will increase your oxygen flow and increase humidity and soothe your eyes, making you feel as though you are getting the benefits of nature. Looking at a plant from nature will help take you back to your most recent forest bathing experience—it may also be beneficial to bring items you collected from the forest into your workspace. A 2014 study done by researchers at the University of Queensland in Australia found evidence that having an office populated with plants made people happier and boosted their productivity by up to 15 percent (Nieuwenhuis et al., 2014).

Listening to recordings of the forest and other natural areas can help place you back into your mindset during forest bathing. When you are stressed and overwhelmed from the tasks of your job, consider listening to natural sounds to calm your nerves. Again, it is important to engage your senses with the forest, whether or not you are physically in it. Various recordings can be found online to help you feel like you are a part of nature. Studies have proven that listening to the sounds of nature provides you with a calming effect and also decreases pain from other health issues; sounds such as that of water flowing was shown to lead to a more positive outlook on work and life, while the sound of birds chirping helped to lower stress (Buxton et al., 2021).

When you have breaks at work, it can be beneficial to go out for walks—or, if you don't have a break, simply looking out of the window at trees and plants can bring you a sense of calm. Taking your lunch break outside is a good way to get away from work stress and to recentre and ground yourself. If there is a park near you, take a walk through it during your break and use all of your senses to take in nature. This will boost serotonin and help you de-stress before you go back to work for the rest of the day, which will improve the quality of the work you do. Research has shown that walking promotes the release of endorphins, which improves your mood when you are stressed or sad (Garden-Robinson, 2011).

Even looking at pictures of natural areas can help you de-stress during the workday. For this reason, you should consider putting pictures of nature at your desk so that you can look at them when you need a second to decompress. Looking at nature brings you a sense of calm, and if you feel overwhelmed and mentally drained while working, having photos ready to look at can be a great help. Research conducted by Vrije University Medical Centre in the Netherlands showed that participants' nerves were settled when they looked at nature photos and their stress levels lowered; the photos supported relaxation and recovery from stressful periods (Dockrill, 2016).

Using natural essential oils at your desk will have the same effect when you use them at your home. Consider bringing a diffuser to work so that you can keep the smell of nature around you at all times. Breathing in these natural scents will give you a feeling of calm, and as discussed before, various essential oils can help you de-stress and improve your mental wellbeing. Essential oils "are a valuable supportive therapy for health and wellness" and can significantly decrease anxiety levels that you may experience when you are overwhelmed by work (Reis and Jones, 2017).

* * *

Working in Nature

Being in the office can be stressful for me, and oftentimes, I find that I am overwhelmed with negative emotions. Since I began forest bathing, I have learned how to improve my work environment to make it a safe, comfortable place where I can still engage in nature. I have bought a peace lily for my desk to have a plant nearby to look at when I get stressed and overwhelmed. While I work, I listen to nature sounds in the background, which gives me great calm when things get too much. I find that I begin to do much better work when I start doing this and that being able to bask myself in the sounds of nature makes my work ethic better. I have decorated my office area with photos of nature that I have visited before. Anytime I feel the need to centre myself, I can look at them and feel calmed by the memories of my forest bathing experiences. At lunchtime, I go to a local park and eat, taking in all of the beautiful scenery around me and appreciating nature for everything that it offers. As I sit and enjoy my lunch, I begin planning my next forest bathing trip in my mind. I imagine where I will go and what I will gain from this trip. I am always learning new things during my forest bathing journeys, and I am excited for what this one will teach me and the lessons that I will bring back to my everyday life.

"Rest is not idleness, and to lie sometimes on the grass under trees on summer's days, listening to the murmur of the water, or watching the clouds float across the sky, is by no means a waste of time." - John Lubbock

* * *

The Future for Us and the Forest

We live in a time where many of our forests around the world are in danger. Forests only cover around 30 percent of the world, and they are quickly disappearing. Between 1990 and 2016, 502,000 square miles of forest were lost—for comparison, this is larger than the entirety of South Africa (Nunez, 2019). Since humans have begun cutting down forests, approximately 46 percent of trees have been felled, and 17 percent of the Amazonian rainforest has been destroyed (Nunez, 2019). Deforestation can be caused by farming, grazing of livestock, mining, drilling, wildfires, and urbanization. In terms of what can be done to slow the process of deforestation, movements and organizations are fighting for ways to preserve existing forest ecosystems and help restore lost trees by planting new ones (Nunez, 2019). Trying to recycle and live sustainably can help slow deforestation more than you may realize, so be mindful of the products you use and use recycled materials whenever possible.

Currently, global biodiversity loss is at an all-time high. The Living Planet Report 2020 found five main threats to biodiversity: land and sea change, pollution, species overexploitation, climate change, and invasive species and disease. Latin America and the Caribbean have lost 94 percent of their biodiversity since 1975 (Living Planet Report, 2020). Biodiversity is essential to maintaining our ecosystem and its functions, making the loss of biodiversity dangerous for the future of our world. Similar to helping deforestation, helping lessen the losses of biodiversity can be done through recycling, buying sustainable materials, and promoting a green way of living. Making an effort to go green and encouraging others to do so is integral to protecting biodiversity and making a change.

Many cultures depend on forests and their benefits. Tribal groups and Indigenous cultures depend on the forest to support their lives. Many tropical rainforests are home to Indigenous peoples, including civilizations like the Mayas, Incas, and Aztecs—civilizations that made huge contributions to science and shaped the environments in which they live ("Rainforest People," 2012). Over one-third of the world's remaining forests are occupied by Indigenous people, and the restoration and protection of forests are essential to these peoples' livelihood—it has also been found that forests under Indigenous management tend to have lower rates of deforestation and emit less carbon dioxide ("Rainforest People," 2012).

Trees provide us with countless benefits, and we must make efforts to slow deforestation. We must work to protect old-growth forests, which have not undergone any major changes as many other forests have. Old-growth forests, besides providing us with the oxygen we need to breathe, hold more wisdom than any forest because of how long they have existed, and they are key to all life on Earth. If we save trees, they will, in turn, save us—their medicine can help us, and they can save the planet while restoring our souls (Plevin, 2019). Though old-growth forests are dwindling because of human greed, we must work to protect them, as there is much wisdom and scientific knowledge to be found from these trees that we have not yet discovered.

The speed at which we are losing our forests negatively impacts our lives and climate change. Deforestation has led to climate change rapidly increasing, and our world is moving towards a dangerous point in time where climate change will become irreversible. Deforestation in the Amazonian forest could potentially be irreversible. The forest's changes could be so severe that the forests may not be able to re-establish if they are destroyed (Shukla et al., 1989). Deforestation has a major impact on climate change—as trees are cleared, their carbon is released into the atmosphere. These emissions make it more difficult to mitigate the rapid growth of climate change (Gorte and Sheikh, 2010). Lowering carbon dioxide emissions is one of the biggest focuses when trying to find ways to mitigate climate change—for this reason, deforestation is becoming increasingly dangerous.

We need to build a relationship with the forest to learn to respect and cherish it. Beyond being important for our livelihood and the health of nature and Earth's climate, forests hold value to helping us mentally and physically. When you practice forest bathing, you are allowed to connect with the forest on a deep level. This connection is crucial to learning how to respect and protect the forest. When you build this relationship, you can understand the true value of the forest.

THE FUTURE FOR US AND THE FOREST

"For most of history, people have had to fight nature to survive; in this century we are beginning to realize that, in order to survive, he must protect it." - Jacques-Yves Cousteau

The Future of Forest Bathing

Forest bathing is beginning to grow in popularity worldwide as doctors recommend it as a type of therapy for patients who suffer from a range of illnesses, including major depression, generalized anxiety, stress, and other mental health issues. For those suffering from high blood pressure and at an increased risk of heart issues, forest bathing can be used as a protective measure. Doctors worldwide are beginning to prescribe forest bathing for other ailments and conditions such as addiction, obesity, and diabetes, as people finally understand the benefits of being in nature and how it can positively impact your health (Li, 2019).

There are organizations dedicated to encouraging forest bathing and strengthening the connection between humans and nature. Forest medicine is now considered a legitimate form of recovery, and organizations are championing forest bathing as a vital practice to maintaining health and wellbeing. The National ParkRx initiative founded in America encourages citizens to use forest bathing to improve their health. There are now more than 150 park-prescription programs that can be found in America through which people can utilize forest medicine. New Zealand encourages a 'green prescription' scheme to help people suffering from the illnesses mentioned above. The National Forest Therapy Centre in South Korea is one of the biggest forest medicine programs in the world, and the South Korean government has spent over $14 million on this centre along with developing thirty-seven state-run recreational forests and training five hundred forest bathing instructors (Li, 2019). The forests in South Korea offer everything you could imagine, and people can live, work, and play through these programs.

What can We Do?

We must preserve both wild and urban forests. Many governments have begun taking measures to protect forests and encourage citizens to protect forests near them and across the world. Preserving urban forests is equally important to preserving our wild forests. Given the decreasing presence of trees in urban environments, we must make some effort to ensure that trees do not disappear from the urban landscape entirely. Trees need to be considered an important part of cities, as they can remove pollution from cities, store tonnes of carbon, and help to mitigate extreme temperatures; they can also help absorb water and excess rainfall while providing relief from noise and dirt, boosting our immune systems, and relieving our stress (Li, 2019). Increasing the presence of trees and other green spaces in urban settings is one of the best things we can do for the environment, and is considered by the World Economic Forum one of the top-ten urban initiatives. Even doing something as simple as planting trees in your backyard can help slow the effects of deforestation. Joining tree planting programs is also a great way of getting involved in preserving forests and trees. Green area protection programs aim to build as many trees as possible and help further preserve green spaces.

Preserving green spaces is not only beneficial for us but is also great for future generations. Children in the city are more disconnected from nature now than ever before. Playing outside will help children become more physically healthy as they get aerobic exercise, build vitamin D levels, improve bone strength, and can help develop a lower risk for chronic illnesses in the future. Children who play outside also develop better cognitively, socially, and emotionally. Children's sensory skills and attention spans are improved if they regularly play outside in nature—and, above all, children who report playing in nature regularly tend to be happier than children who do not (Lund, 2018). By connecting our children with forests now, we can help them grow up to know how to protect them—and the cycle will continue.

THE FUTURE FOR US AND THE FOREST

"The creation of a thousand forests is in one acorn." - *Ralph Waldo Emerson*

Sharing is Caring

Nature helps us learn how to share and support others. Nature itself shares with us, and understanding nature's sustainable system helps us know how to share with others. Older trees pass on nutrients to young seedlings, giving them a chance to grow bigger and stronger. The oldest, biggest trees can send food and warnings to their surrounding trees and share nutrients across various species. One example of this is how, in winter, when aspens are weaker, conifers pass along food to allow the aspens to stay healthy (Plevin, 2019). In addition to this, if insects attack one tree, it instinctively distributes chemicals through the underground network to warn surrounding trees of a potential attack, giving them the ability to defend themselves (Plevin, 2019).

We can adopt the lessons from trees in our own lives, learning to support one another. We can use the networks we have built to strengthen our relationships and share with others. Share with the ones you love everything you have learned from the forest—share the practice of forest bathing with your family and friends and encourage them to join you on your next adventure. Similar to how nature shares with everything around it, we can give and share to those we love.

"If you will stay close to nature, to its simplicity, to the small things hardly noticeable, those things can unexpectedly become great and immeasurable." - Rainer Maria Rilke

Final Words

Forest bathing is one of the best methods of self-improvement and self-care that you can practice. Through forest bathing, I have become what I believe to be the best version of myself. Beyond the health benefits that forest bathing provides, it is a way to connect with myself and the world around me. I have never felt as in tune with nature as I do when sitting in the forest, taking in the surrounding beauty. Forest bathing gives me the chance to unwind, de-stress, and recognize how precious life is. The history of forest bathing is beautiful and intricate, and the long-used practice has helped me in ways I never could have imagined. I am a healthier person, physically and mentally, and I owe forest bathing my thanks for that.

Nature holds more power than we realize. Trees have the power to restore us, and forest bathing can be used as a therapy method to help any aching souls. Prepare yourself for the internal journey you will embark upon when forest bathing. You will likely discover things about yourself that you didn't know before and that, in many ways, you will find yourself through this experience. Notice everything and anything that you feel during your journey, and keep track of your emotions. Take this time to disconnect—work, life, anything else stressing you out doesn't matter. All of life's stressors go away when you fully immerse yourself in the forest and the world around you. Find the place that connects with you the most—whether it is a forest, a park, or simply your backyard, the value of forest bathing cannot be understated.

Use forest bathing as a way to connect with your senses and open your eyes to your sixth sense. Connecting fully with your senses opens your eyes to the beauty of the surrounding world—beauty that you may have never realized before. When you are in nature, let it guide you. Nature will protect and comfort you, and you should put all of your trust and faith into this experience. If nature guides you in a certain direction, trust that this is the direction you need to go in so that you can find yourself.

Foster your relationship with nature by creating your own forest. This not only benefits you but benefits the environment, which is suffering from a crisis that we need to reverse before it is too late. Planting your own trees and creating a home for yourself can be life-changing. Any way to create your own forest is valuable and deepens your connection with the world around you.

Throughout this book, you have begun to learn why forest bathing is so important and how it can help change your life. There is no better time than now to begin your forest bathing journey. No matter any doubts you may still have or reservations you may feel, it is important that you try—even if it is not a success at first, you will learn how to be in tune with nature and everything surrounding you. You will find immense value in your time forest bathing, and you will see nature in a way that you never have before.

If you are hesitant, take the leap and explore the world. Once you are in your rhythm, you will only have one question: why wasn't I doing this all along?

Moss & Pine Book Club

Thank you for joining me on my forest bathing practice - I hope you found the book inspiring and feel empowered to embark on your own forest bathing journey.

If you loved the book and have a minute to spare, I would really appreciate a short review on the page or site where you bought the book. Your help in spreading the word is greatly appreciated. Reviews from readers like you make a huge difference in helping new readers to connect with nature.

Thank you so much!

Nic Aiden and the Moss & Pine team

P.S. If you'd like to know when other new nature and adventure inspired books are coming out and want to receive occasional updates, then you can sign up and join the Moss & Pine Book Club here: www.mossandpine.net

Alternatively, you can follow us on Instagram or Facebook for the latest news and book releases: @mossandpinepress

References

Agarwal, S., Bhartiya, S., Mithal, K., Shukla, P., & Dabas, G. (2021). Increase in ocular problems During COVID-19 pandemic in school going Children- a survey based study. *Indian Journal of Ophthalmology*, *69*(3), 777–778. https://doi.org/10.4103/ijo.ijo_2981_20

Buxton, R. T., Pearson, A. L., Allou, C., Fristrup, K., & Wittemyer, G. (2021). A synthesis of health benefits of natural sounds and their distribution in national parks. *Proceedings of the National Academy of Sciences*, *118*(14). https://doi.org/10.1073/pnas.2013097118

CDC. (2021, January 11). *Poor nutrition*. Centers for Disease Control and Prevention. Retrieved September 26, 2021, from https://www.cdc.gov/chronicdisease/resources/publications/factsheets/nutrition.htm.

Cohen, S., Kamarck, T., & Mermelstein, R. (1983). A global measure of perceived stress. *Journal of Health and Social Behavior*, *24*(4), 385. https://doi.org/10.2307/2136404

Cournoyer, C., & Fetterman, M. (2018, April 16). *What cities and states are doing to cut noise, 'the new secondhand smoke'*. Governing. Retrieved September 23, 2021, from https://w

ww.governing.com/archive/sl-noise-pollution.html.

Davis, C. (2012, April 10). *Three similarities between trees and humans*. Frank Miller Lumber. Retrieved September 19, 2021, from https://frankmiller.com/three-similarities-between-trees-and-humans/.

Dearmont, C. (n.d.). *How blue light affects mental health*. Mental Health America. Retrieved September 24, 2021, from https://mhanational.org/blog/how-blue-light-affects-mental-health.

Dong, K., Goyarts, E. C., Pelle, E., Trivero, J., & Pernodet, N. (2019). Blue light disrupts the circadian rhythm and create damage in skin cells. International Journal of Cosmetic Science, 41(6), 558–562. https://doi.org/10.1111/ics.12572

Garden-Robinson, J. (2011, August 8). *Walking can help relieve stress*. NDSU. Retrieved September 29, 2021, from https://www.ag.ndsu.edu/news/newsreleases/2011/aug-8-2011/walking-can-help-relieve-stress/.

Gascon M, Mas MT, Martínez D, Dadvand P, Forns J, Plasència A, et al. *Mental health benefits of long-term exposure to residential green and blue spaces: A systematic review*. Int J Environ Res Public Health. 2015 Apr 1;12(4):4354–79.

Gladwell, V. F., Brown, D. K., Wood, C., Sandercock, G. R., & Barton, J. L. (2013, January 3). *The great outdoors: How a green exercise environment can benefit all*. Extreme Physiology & Medicine. Retrieved September 29, 2021, from https://doi.org

/10.1186/2046-7648-2-3.

Göransson, A. (2021, February 16). *Tackling the issue of noise pollution in Smart Cities*. Secure Insights. Retrieved September 23, 2021, from https://www.axis.com/blog/secure-insights/noise-pollution-smart-cities/.

Gorte, R. W., & Sheikh, P. A. (2010). Deforestation and climate change.

Holzman, D. C. (2010). What's in a color? The unique human health effects of blue light. *Environmental Health Perspectives, 118*(1). https://doi.org/10.1289/ehp.118-a22

Iora Health Inc. (2020, June 8). *Health benefits of herbal tea for a healthy lifestyle*. Iora Primary Care. Retrieved September 29, 2021, from https://ioraprimarycare.com/blog/herbal-tea-benefits/.

Kawakami, K., Kawamoto, M., Nomura, M., Otani, H., Nabika, T., & Gonda, T. (2004). Effects of Phytoncides on Blood Pressure under Restraint Stress in Shrsp. *Clinical & Experimental Pharmacology & Physiology, 31,* S27-S28.

Koster, J., McElreath, R., Hill, K., Yu, D., Shepard, G., van Vliet, N., Gurven, M., Trumble, B., Bird, R. B., Bird, D., Codding, B., Coad, L., Pacheco-Cobos, L., Winterhalder, B., Lupo, K., Schmitt, D., Sillitoe, P., Franzen, M., Alvard, M., … Ross, C. (2020). The life history of human foraging: Cross-cultural and individual variation. *Science Advances, 6*(26). https://doi.org/10.1126/sciadv.aax9070

Kotera, Y., Richardson, M., & Sheffield, D. (2020). Effects of Shinrin-Yoku (Forest Bathing) and Nature Therapy on Mental Health: a Systematic Review and Meta-analysis. *International Journal of Mental Health & Addiction,* 1-25.

Lee, J., & Allen, J. (2021). Gender Differences in Healthy and Unhealthy Food Consumption and Its Relationship with Depression in Young Adulthood. Community Mental Health Journal, 57(5), 898–909. https://doi.org/10.1007/s10597-020-00672-x

Li, Q. (2018, May 1). *The benefits of 'forest bathing'.* Time. Retrieved September 11, 2021, from https://time.com/5259602/japanese-forest-bathing/.

Li, Q. (2019). *Into the forest: How trees can help you find health and happiness.* Penguin Life, an imprint of Penguin Books.

Li, Q., Kobayashi, M., Kumeda, S., Ochiai, T., Miura, T., Kagawa, T., Imai, M., Wang, Z., Otsuka, T., & Kawada, T. (2016). Effects of Forest Bathing on Cardiovascular and Metabolic Parameters in Middle-Aged Males. *Evidence-based complementary and alternative medicine : eCAM, 2016,* 2587381. https://doi.org/10.1155/2016/2587381

Lund, D. (2018, June 26). *Top 5 benefits of children playing outside.* Sanford Health News. Retrieved October 1, 2021, from https://news.sanfordhealth.org/childrens/play-outside/.

Michell, A. (2020, February 6). *Chocolate Oat Bran Muffins.* Plant Based And Broke. Retrieved September 28, 2021, from https://plantbasedandbroke.com/chocolate-oat-bran-muffins-vegan-gluten-free/.

Mongabay. (2012, July 31). *Who lives in the rainforest?*Mongabay.com. Retrieved September 29, 2021, from https://rainforests.mongabay.com/0701.htm.

Nieuwenhuis, M., Knight, C., Postmes, T., & Haslam, S. A. (2014). The relative benefits of green versus Lean office Space: Three field experiments. *Journal of Experimental Psychology: Applied, 20*(3), 199–214. https://doi.org/10.1037/xap0000024

Nunez, K. (2020, November 9). *Breath of fire yoga: Benefits and how to do it correctly*. Healthline. Retrieved September 25, 2021, from https://www.healthline.com/health/breath-of-fire-yoga.

Ober, C., Sinatra, S., Zucker, M. (2014). Earthing: The Most Important Health Discovery Ever!. *Laguna Beach, CA: Basic Health Publications*

Payne, M.D., & Delphinus, E. (2019). A Review of the Current Evidence for the Health Benefits Derived from Forest Bathing. *International Journal of Health, Wellness & Society, 9*(1), 19-30.

Pizer, A. (2020, June 30). *Easily learn ujjayi breath to deepen your yoga practice*. Verywell Fit. Retrieved September 25, 2021, from https://www.verywellfit.com/ocean-breath-ujjayi-pranayama-3566763.

Plevin, J. (2018). From haiku to shinrin-yoku: a brief history of forest bathing. *Forest History Today*, (Spring/Fall 2018), 17–19.

Plevin, J. (2019). *Healing magic of forest bathing: Finding calm, creativity, and connection in the natural world*. Ten Speed Press.

Quinn, D. (2021, January 20). *Foot reflexology Chart: Points, how to, benefits, and risks*. Healthline. Retrieved September 26, 2021, from https://www.healthline.com/health/foot-reflexology-chart.

Rashan, L., Hakkim, F., Idrees, M., Essa, M., Velusamy, T., Al-Baloshi, M., Al-Balushi, B., Al Jabri, A., Al-Rizeiqi, M., Guillemin, G., & Abdo Hasson, S. S. (2019). Boswellia Gum Resin and Essential Oils: Potential Health Benefits – An Evidence-Based Review. International Journal of Nutrition, Pharmacology, Neurological Diseases, 9(2), 53–71. https://doi.org/10.4103/ijnpnd.ijnpnd_11_19

Reis, D., & Jones, T. (2017). Aromatherapy: Using essential oils as a supportive therapy. *Clinical Journal of Oncology Nursing*, *21*(1). https://doi.org/10.1188/17.cjon.16-19

Sackett, C. (2010). Ecotherapy: A Counter to Society's Unhealthy Trend? Journal of Creativity in Mental Health, 5(2), 134–141. https://doi.org/10.1080/15401383.2010.485082

Shukla, J., Nobre, C., & Sellers, P. (1990). Amazon deforestation and climate change. *Science*, *247*(4948), 1322-1325.

Singh, A. (n.d.). *Surya bhedana Pranayama (Right NOSTRIL Breathing)-Steps and benefits*. Sarvyoga. Retrieved September 25, 2021, from https://www.sarvyoga.com/.

Slater, V. (2018, May 15). *How and why to use essential oils.* Ohio State Medical Center. Retrieved September 29, 2021, from https://wexnermedical.osu.edu/blog/essential-oils.

Spritzler, F. (2021, May 19). *21 reasons to eat real food.* Healthline. Retrieved September 26, 2021, from https://www.healthline.com/nutrition/21-reasons-to-eat-real-food#TOC_TITLE_HDR_15.

Tomer, J. (2011). What Causes Obesity? And Why Has It Grown So Much? *Challenge, 54*(4), 22–49.

Torgovnick May, K. (2012, July 10). *6 great things microbes do for US.* TED Blog. Retrieved September 15, 2021, from https://blog.ted.com/6-great-things-microbes-do-for-us/.

Ulrich, R. (1984). View through a window may influence recovery from surgery. *Science, 224*(4647), 420–421. https://doi.org/10.1126/science.6143402

West, H. (2019, September 30). *What are essential oils, and do they work?* Healthline. Retrieved September 24, 2021, from https://www.healthline.com/nutrition/what-are-essential-oils.

W.L. Gore & Associates. (2017, November 8). *Foraging for beginners: Tips for safely gathering wild, edible foods.* Retrieved September 28, 2021, from https://www.gore-tex.com/blog/foraging-food-wild-plants.

World Wide Fund For Nature. (2020). *Living Planet Report 2020.*